# Political Question and Article 356

# Political Question and Article 356

Dr. P. Rathnaswamy

1998

Manas Publications

New Delh-10002

MANAS PUBLICATIONS
4819/XI, Varun House, Mathur Lane,
24, Ansari Road, Darya Ganj,
New Delhi-110002 (INDIA)
Ph.: 3260783, 3265523, 2919762, 2523865
Fax : 011 - 3272766 & 2927854
E-Mail : manas.vkgarg@axcess.net.in



ISBN 81-7049-083-9



First Published 1998

*Typeset at*
Innovative Processors
New Delhi-110 002

*Printed in India at*
Santosh Offset, Delhi
and Published by Mrs. Suman Lata for
Manas Publications, 4819/XI, Varun House,
Mathur Lane, 24, Ansari Road, Darya Ganj,
New Delhi-110002 (INDIA)

# Preface

The Doctrine of Political Question has been in the discussion before the Supreme Court of United States of America until a beginning was made in Marbury vs. Madison. The issue had been discussed in subsequent cases, Cohens vs. Virginia (1821), Rescue Army vs. Municipal Court of Los Angeles (1947), Baker vs. Carr (1962) Powell vs. McCormack (1969) United States vs. Nixon (1974), Goldwater vs. Cartar (1979) and Nixon vs. United States (1993). In all these cases two divergent views have been developed. The first view is that the political question doctrine is beyond the jurisdiction of the judiciary. The second view is that it is within the competence of judiciary. In the case of Nixon vs. United States 1993, the Court held that it was a non-justiciable political question unlike in the case of United States vs. Nixon 1974. In India, the Political Question Doctrine has slowly emerged as it is subject to judicial review in the Rajasthan case, the Bommai's case etc. The emerged view of India is clearer than in USA.

The Political Question is a zone, which divides non-justiciable political question from justiciable political question. The judiciary has slowly consolidated its decisions to bring a definite interpretation to the concept of political question. It has solved many problems.

There is another fact, which demonstrates that, removing the distinction between non-justiciable political question and justiciable political question has failed to evoke sufficient authority and clarity. This is not simple classification or codification but it is to provide constitutionalism. Separation of Powers is not the subject to deliberate. The intentions of the founding fathers are rearranged because of failure or because of otherwise and this is to be seen.

In India, the Doctrine of non-justiciable political question has been from the British legacy as established in Government of India Act, 1919 and 1935. This has continued until recently in the Indian constitution. Now, the views are changed. The discussion in this book is specifically focussed on emergency provisions particularly the President rule under Article 356. The discussion has been arranged historically and to the latest cases also. Shri HM Seervai has discussed the pros and cons of emergency provisions and ultimately he has opted for deletion of the emergency provisions from the constitution of India. Many political leaders advocated for the abolition of Article 356. Even today, there are two views. One view is against Article 356 and another view is for Article 356.

In this book various options are discussed in this regard. The author is for the Article 356 and not for the omission of it. In order to create additional safeguards against abuse of Article 356, he has suggested certain solutions. The political question is a doctrine which cannot be simply placed into either justiciable political question or non-justiciable political question but it needs to be understood in totality and not in isolation. The American experience has not been very concrete and consistent because there is lack of consistency and lack of understanding of it by treating it in isolation. Indian judiciary has brilliantly understood it but however, there is more in the process or reaching perfection. This book teaches the reasons for understanding this subject in totality and not in isolation. It is a good book for constitutional practitioner and as well as students of law.

I would like to acknowledge my thanks to the publisher for timely publication and my Personal Assistants who have been instrumental in bringing out this book. But for my wife it would not have been possible.

**Dr. P. Rathnaswamy**

# *Contents*

# 1

# *Introduction*

The Supreme Court in the case of S.R. Bommai and Others etc etc vs Union of India and Others etc etc. held in its Judgment on 11.3.1994 that Article 356 of the Constitution confers upon the President of India a conditional power and not absolute power.

Art 356 confers a power upon the President of India only to be exercised when he is satisfied that a situation has arisen where the govt of a state cannot be carried on in accordance with the provisions of the constitution. Article 356 confers power upon the President of India to impose President's Rule on a State under the circumstances mentioned above. It is also held that the material existence on the above condition of Government of a State can not be carried out in accordance with the provisions of the constitution including the reports of the Governor of the State are a precondition. While interpreting the provisions of article 356 (1) the court held that the power of dissolving the Legislative Assembly could be exercised by the President in the approval of the Parliament by both the houses on the proposal of dissolving Legislative Assembly and until then the power of the President of India is only available to suspend the legislative assembly. The Court has also held that under these circumstances there could not be two Governments according to Article 356 (1). In other words certain functions of the State can not be taken over by the President while leaving the remaining functions with the state government. Under these circumstances for certain functions there is government under the wisdom of President of India and another Government is by the state government itself. Therefore while invoking the provision of constitution article 356 (1) there should be only one government and which is the government as per the President's proclamation under article 356. The honorable court while reviewing the provision of article 356 (3) held that if the proclamation is not approved by the Parliament by both the Houses within two months and acts of the state government viz. order ussing by passed the during the period of the two months do not get invalidated or do not become illegal since the proclamation lapses. As the legislative assembly is suspended the legislative assembly is revived resulting into the revival of the State Government. If the proclamation order is approved by the both the houses of Parliament the legislative assembly stands dissolved and on the subsequent lapse of proclamation order the dissolved assembly does not revive. According to Article 74 (2) the advise rendered by the council of ministers to the President on the dissolution of the Legislative Assembly or proclamation of President's rule can be claimed as a privileged document invoking section 123 of Evidence Act. However the decision to claim the particular document as a privileged document under Section 123 of Evidence Act is subject to the scrutiny of the court. The hon'ble court can take a decision on its merits. At the same time the court will not go into the details of the correctness of the material or its adequacy. The proclamation order under article 356 (1) is not immune from judicial review. At the same time if the court has the power to strike down the proclamation it has also the power to restore the displaced govt. to office and reactivate the legislative assembly wherever it may have dissolved or kept under suspension. Under such circumstances the court has the power to declare that acts done, order passed and laws made during the period the proclamation was in force shall remain unaffected and be treated as valid.

The proclamation dated April 21, 1989, in respect of Karnataka and the proclamation dated October 11, 1991, in respect of Meghalaya are unconstitutional. If the fresh elections have not taken place and the new governments not formed the court would have revived the dissolved assemblies and restored the respective governments. The proclamation dated Jan 15, 1993 in respect of Madhya Pradesh, Rajasthan and Himachal Pradesh are not unconstitutional.

The judgement of Hon'ble Supreme Court in this case is by nine judges constitution bench.

By virtue of this judgement certain basic questions have been answered permanently. The first question is the judicial power of the court to declare the proclamation constitutional or unconstitutional. This power is the power of judicial review. The second question which has been answered is that if the proclamation is held unconstitutional the court has the power to revive the dissolved legislative assembly and restore the state government. The third question that has been answered is that even if the proclamation is approved by both the Houses of Parliament within the period of two months the court has the power to revive the dissolved legislative assembly and restore the government when the Court holds the Proclamation unconstitutional. The fourth question that has been answered is that the President has the conditional power under article 356 (1) and there is no absolute power vested in him. Like any other document, the document claimed under article 74 (2), the exemption under the category of privileged document invoking section 123 of Evidence Act, is subject to judicial review of the court.

By virtue of this judgement the court has started its supremacy over the presidential power under article 356. This is bringing the Constitutional law equivalent to any other Law or legislation. According to the power of amendment to the constitution there are some of the provisions and for schedule 7 of the constitution for other classes of amendment there are other procedures. If the constitution law is treated at par with any other ordinary law there is no need of maintaining a separate procedure for various provisions in the constitution.

If the judgment of the Supreme Court of 1994 in the case of S R Bommai and Others is accepted there needs to be a reconsideration on the merit of sustaining separate procedures for invoking amendments to various provisions. Similarly by virtue of equating constitution law with any other law the power of judicial review is not only expanded but it has destroyed the basic classifications and procedural differentiation towards the procedure to amendment to the constitution. In such a case either the procedure to amend the constitution has to be modified so that there is no distinction in the procedures while amendment to the constitution is effected. Similarly the power of writ jurisdiction that has been restricted only to high courts and Supreme Court should be eliminated so that each court has the same power. In other words equating certain specific provisions of the constitution with any other law is as demoralizing as removing the special status of high court and Supreme Court in respect of writ jurisdiction.

Recently, the President's proclamation was in continuity in U P despite the fact the election to the legislative assembly was completed. The Parliament has also passed the resolution on extension of President's Rule in U. P. beyond the period of six months but however the newly elected legislative assembly has been in existence without dissolution or without taking oath of newly elected legislative assembly Members. The non formation of the government in U.P is due to the fact that no party has enjoyed the majority to form the government or no combination of or coalition of parties could successfully form as a forum to form the government resulting in a position of impasse. Neither has there been any dissolution of assembly nor the new Government is formed. This is a typical situation and it involves a political question and not a mere judicial interpretation. Subsequently BJP and BSP formed a coalition government and these two parties have been called in by the governor of Uttar Pradesh to form the government and to prove the majority on the floor of the House. The Speaker was elected and oath by the newly elected members was taken. The solution to the problem here again has been found by a political decision where neither there is elected government nor the dissolution of the house. Such considerations cannot be taken inside the chambers of judiciary. This does not mean that the judiciary must be a silent spectator where there is illegal and unlawful proclamation. It has to be tactfully perceived and a decision has to be taken.

In America, the Supreme Court has undergone a series of changes until it has established a power of judicial review. The power of judicial review has been looked at in different dimensions. The political scientists are of the opinion that the court is weak and it is under the control of political branches. In other words the judgement of the court is overruled or nullified by bringing an amendment or by brining a new legislation. Similarly the judges are appointed as per the wisdom of political branches of government. If the Parliament or the legislative body aims to bring down the number of judges or increase the number of judges the balance of judges could be dealt in either way. The Parliament can remove the justices in accordance with the constitutional provisions. Therefore the judiciary is weak and is under the control of political branches. Under such circumstances to protect the people and its own position it needs active branches. This is possible by virtue of judicial review. The power of judicial review needs to be expanded depending upon the need and necessity. The judicial power of the court is made dynamic through the expansion of judicial review. Removal of judicial review is nothing but elimination of judicial power.

Therefore, the political question needs to be studied keeping in view the importance of judicial review. The political question should not become a substitute to the judicial review and at the same time the judicial review should not replace the relevence of political question. These aspects will be discussed in this book in detail.

# 2

# Historical Introduction

*Historical Introduction to the adoption of Article 356 in our Federal Scheme - The Government of India Act, 1935 - Constituent Assembly Debates on Draft of Article 356*

The Indian Constitution is basically an instrumental compromise initiated and evolved by the British Empire during the 200 years rule over India and in the process it has given birth to so many Government of India Acts and Legislations .These legislations and constitutional practice of British empire in conjunction with infant democratic aspirations during the 1950s of Indian independence struggle have given birth to Constitution of India. This is evident that the constitutional provisions of Government of India Act, 1935 are reflected in the Constitution of India. Therefore, it will be appropriate to look back at the British Executive Functions before studying the role of governor and the President of India in reference to presidential proclamation under article 356.

The executive functions are discussed at Page No. 15 of *'The Principles of British Constitutional Law'* authored by Cecil S. Emden, published by Methuen & Co. Ltd., 36 Essex Street W.C., London in 1925.

## 2.1 EXECUTIVE FUNCTIONS

The functions exercised by the British Executive which conform to the standard adopted may be divided as follows :-

(i) Conduct of intercourse with other States, and with other parts of the empire, including the negotiation of treaties;
(ii) provision for defence against aggression;
(iii) declaration and conduct of war, and making of peace;
(iv) summoning and dissolving the legislature;
(v) initiation of legislation (concurrently with legislatures);
(vi) execution of the laws of the land through the administrative' departments (including the appointment to offices in those departments);
(vii) maintenance of order and improvement of social and economic conditions;
(viii) pardon.

In the case of more than one of the above particular functions the exercise is subject to a check by the legislature or the judiciary. This position does not prevent the functions being those of the Executive." p.15 ibid

## 2.2 OTHER INSTANCES OF PRIMARY LEGISLATION

The Executive, through the agency of the Privy Council, can, in addition to its powers of legislation in respect of Dominions overseas, issue legislative regulations by order in Council for the government of the Army and Navy ("King's Regulations"), for the government of the Civil Service (1); and it is probably still possible for the Executive to regulate trade and commerce in time of war by Order in Council, and to make proclamations at the time of war prohibiting persons from leaving the realm - all these without reference to the legislature.

## 2.3 SECONDARY LEGISLATION

Another function of the Executive which does not conform to standard is also legislative; but, unlike that just noticed, it is exercised subject to the authority of the legislature. It is described as delegated, secondary or subordinate legislation; and it becomes necessary in two sets of circumstances. First, because emergencies occur in the life of all states; and, since the legislature is not in permanent session and is not, even if it is in session, by its size and structure fitted to deal effectively with a sudden situation, the Executive has delegated to it powers of issuing the necessary decree. And secondly, because, in a highly developed and thickly populated state of any magnitude, the task of government becomes specialised and complicated to an extent which disables any legislature from exercising the whole of the legislative function. Difficulties of this nature were even experienced in ancient Athens. acquing degree specialisation, a double exercise of functions followed.

Emphasis must be laid on the facts (i) that the Executive must strictly observe the limits of its authorisation; and, if it exceeds them, it is liable to be checked through the judiciary) below), and (ii) that there is no general authorisation to the Executive to issue ordinances to carry out the purposes of statutes. In order to make the executive to issue ordinances for the execution of a statute, the statute must contain express provision. In this latter respect there is a contrast with the constitutional position in some foreign countries. In France, although the Executive is expressly given power to issue regulations to execute statutes, it has a general power to issue decrees to fill in the gaps which are left in statutes drawn in general terms. The position appears to be somewhat similar under the German Constitution (of 1919) which provides (Chap.I, Sect.V, Art.77, that "The National Cabinet issues the general administrative regulations necessary for the execution of the national laws so far as the laws do not otherwise provide ..." But other constitutions, like the Serbian (of 1921) (Art.94), provision that there must be a distinct "legal authorisation" in each case.

## 2.4 SECONDARY LEGISLATION IN EMERGENCIES

Some system of delegation in case of emérgency is a necessity which has been generally appreciated. As an example of comparative interest an article of the Japanese constitution may serve (Chap.I, Art.8) : "The Emperor, in consequence of an urgent necessity to maintain public safety or to avert public calamities, issues, when the Imperial Diet is not sitting, Imperial ordinances in the place of laws. Such Imperial ordinances are to be laid before the Imperial Diet at its next session, and when the Diet does not approve the said ordinances the government shall declare them to be invalid for the future."

In England there was an "early and isolated phase," in the reign of Henry VIII, in which authority was given to the Executive to deal by delegated legislation with urgent situations. This phase is largely attributable to the political machinations of the Sovereign of that time, and does not bear appreciably on the position today. There may, therefore, simply be noted the statute of 31 Hen.8, c.8, which empowered the King to issue proclamations to be obeyed

The chief instances of similar legislation during the immediately succeeding centuries were connected with emergencies due to threats of disease. By the statute of 9 Anne, c.2, authority was given to the Executive to issue regulations in view of the prevalent plague, so as to enforce quarantine" in a more expeditious manner than at present can be in the ordinary methods of the law." A later example is the delegation under the Contagious Diseases of Animals Act, 1848 (1).

In the war of 1914-18 it became necessary in Great Britain to pass statutes giving the Executive special powers of issuing delegated legislation, so as to protect national interests; and it was felt after the conclusion of the war that there should be permanent statutory authority for the Executive to issue ordinances in the event of urgent situations of other kinds. There was accordingly passed the Emergency Powers Act, 1920(2).

1. 11 & 12 Vict. c.105, ss. 105, 107. These examples are taken from Carr, "Delegated Legislation," pp.22-26.

2. 10 & 11 Geo. 5, c. 55.

This Act provides (section I (1)) for the issue of a proclamation of emergency, if it appears "that any action has been by any persons or body of persons of such a nature and on so extensive a scale to be calculated, by with the supply and distribution of food, water, fuel, or light, or with the means of locomotion, to deprive the community, or any substantial portion of the community, of the essentials of life."

In the case of the issue of a proclamation of emergency, provision is made for the early meeting of Parliament, if it is not sitting at the time (section I (2)), and for the making of regulations by order in Council (section 2 (I)) " for securing the essentials of life to the community." These regulations may confer or impose upon a government department such powers and duties as may be deemed "necessary for the preservation of the peace, for securing and regulating the supply and distribution of food, water, fuel, light, and other necessities, for maintaining the means of transit or locomotion, and for any other purposes essential to the public safety and the life of the community."

The considerable extent of the powers of a legislative nature conferred on the Executive by this act are sufficient and special attention needs only be drawn to the capacity of the Executive to alter the criminal law for seven days without any check by Parliament, There were the special powers on emergency in order to keep the govt. his continuity so as to avoid any revolution or strong and deep resentment by the people. Such acts lead to the discussion of political question which is more complicated but very clear to the aims. These aspects are discussed here.

## 2.5 SPECIAL RESPONSIBILITIES

The Federal and Provincial executives differ, however, on a number of important respects.

First, the executive authority of each province only extends to the matters with respect to which the Legislature of the province has power to make laws.

Secondly, in the exercise of his functions the Governor of a province has the following special responsibilities -

(a) the prevention of any grave menace to the peace or tranquillity of the province or any part there of;

(b) the safeguarding of the legitimate interests of minorities;

(c) the securing to, and to the dependents of, persons who are or have been members of the public services of any rights provided or preserved for them by or under this act, and the safeguarding of their legitimate interests;

(d) the securing in the sphere of executive action of the purposes which the provisions of Chapter III of Part V of the act (which deals with discrimination) are designed to secure in relation to legislation;

(e) the securing of the peace and good government of areas which by or under the provisions of the Act are declared to be partially excluded areas;

(f) the protection of the rights of any Indian State and the rights and dignity of the ruler thereof; and

(g) the securing of the execution of orders or directions lawfully issued to him under Part VI of the act (which deals with administrative relations) by the Governor-General in his discretion.

It should be noted that a Governor, unlike the Governor-General, has no special responsibility for -

(1) the safeguarding of the financial stability and credit of either the Federal Government or his province;

(2) the prevention of action which would subject the goods of United Kingdom or Burmese origin imported into India to discriminatory or penal treatment;

(3) the securing of the due discharge of functions with respect to reserved subjects.

The governor's special responsibility for securing the execution of orders lawfully issued by the Governor-General was included in order to ensure that whenever the Governor-General desired to exercise powers which required the co-operation of provincial administrations the Governors should be in a position to give effect to any directions or orders of the Governor-General to this effect, even if the execution of any such directions or orders was not acceptable to their own ministers.

## 2.6 CRIMES OF VIOLENCE

A third difference between the Federal and provincial executives arises from the fact that the Act does not reserve any subjects for the consideration of the governors. The Act, however, provides that -

57 - (1) If it appears to the governor of a province that the peace or tranquillity of the province is endangered by the operations of any persons committing, or conspiring, preparing or attempting to commit, crimes of violence which, in the opinion of the governor, are intended to overthrow the government as by law established, the governor may, if he thinks that the circumstances of the case require him to do so for the purpose of combating those operations, direct that his functions shall, to such extent as may be specified in the direction, be exercised by him in his discretion and, until otherwise provided by a subsequent direction of the governor, those functions shall to that extent be exercised by him accordingly.

If Governor decides to exercise this power, he is further authorised, at his own discretion, to appoint an official as a temporary member of the legislature to act as his mouthpiece in that body, and any official so appointed has the same powers and rights, other than the power to vote, as an elected member.

The powers given to the governors under section 57 are powers which are over and above their special responsibility for the prevention of any grave menace to peace and tranquillity and were conferred, according to the report of the Joint Select Committee, in order to ensure that the measures taken to deal with terrorism and other activities of revolutionary conspirators should not be less efficient and unhesitating under the act than they have been in the past.

In order to further this object, section 58 provides that the Governors, in their discretion, shall make rules for securing that no records or information relating to the intelligence service dealing with terrorism are to be disclosed to anyone other than such persons within the provincial police forces as the inspector-generals or the commissioners of police may direct, or such other public officers outside those forces as the governors themselves may direct.

## 2.7 IMMUNITY FROM PROCEEDINGS

Section 306 confers upon the Governor-General, the governors and the Secretary of State a certain legal immunity. No proceedings whatsoever are to lie in, and no process is to issue from any court in India against these officers of State, whether in a personal capacity or otherwise, in respect of anything done or omitted to be done by them in the performance or purported performance of their duties. After retirement this immunity from legal proceedings in Indian courts is to continue. Since, however, there may be extreme cases in which it would be desirable to remove this protection. The section provides that actions may be initiated against these officers after retirement if the sanction of His Majesty in council has been previously obtained. This section, of course, does not restrict the right of any person to bring against the Federation, a province or the Secretary of State similar to the provisions in Chapter III of Part VII of the Act, which deal with property, contracts and suits.

It should be noticed that this section only applies to proceedings in Indian courts. At common law the Governor of any territories of the Crown is liable to an action for damages both in the courts of those territories and in the Court of King's Bench in England for acts done in his private and unofficial capacity. In Hill v. Brigg (1841, 3 Moo. P.C.C. 465), it was held that a colonial court could try an action of debt to which the Governor was a party. In Mostyn v. Fabrigas (1774, 20 State Tr. 81) a petition of an alleged mutinous character was presented to the Governor of Minorca by one Fabrigas, who was later imprisoned. It was held that the Court of King's Bench in England could entertain an action for false imprisonment against the Governor. In Musgrove v Pulido (1879, 5 App. Cas, 111) it was decided that a Governor could be sued in England for acts done in his official capacity, but outside the limits of his authority. Hence it follows that section

306 only derogates from the common law rule in so far as it restricts the right to bring proceedings in Indian Courts.

The Government of India Act 1915 dealt with certain criminal offences committed by any person holding office under the Crown in India; for example, under section 124 of that Act any servant of the Crown who, within his jurisdiction or in the exercise of his authority, oppressed any British subject was guilty of a misdemeanor. This Act has been repealed and the new constitution act does not contain provisions of a similar nature. In these circumstances it follows that Governors and other servants of the Crown in India must be tried in the Court of King's Bench in England for misconduct under the joint operation of the Governors Act 1699 (11 & 12 Will. III, c. 12) and the Criminal Jurisdiction Act 1802 (42 Geo.III, c.85). The Governors Act 1699 provides that Governors may be tried "for acts of oppression within the area of their command, or for any other crime or offence contrary to the laws of the realm or in force within their respective governments or commands". The Act of 1802 extended the Governors Act to all servants of the Crown.

In 1802 Governor Wall was tried at the Old Bailey, convicted, sentenced and executed for causing the death of one Benjamin Armstrong by the infliction of excessive corporal punishment. In R.V.Eyre (L.R. 3 Q.B. 487) it was held that where a colonial governor has been found guilty of crime in his official capacity the Court of King's Bench, either upon information by the Attorney-General or indictment found by the grand jury, may try such crime, and such crime may be said to have been committed in Middlesex.

## 2.8 A STATE OF EMERGENCY

It was perceived that it might be advisable for the Federal Legislature to possess a residuary power at a time of crisis. Accordingly, section 102 provides that, if the Governor-General has at his discretion declared proclamation that a grave emergency exists whereby the security of India is threatened and whether by war or internal disturbance, the Federal legislature is to have power to make laws for a province with respect to any of the matters enumerated in the provincial legislative list. A proviso adds that no Bill or amendment for these purposes is to be introduced or moved without the previous sanction of the Governor-General. Before giving his sanction, the Governor-General should satisfy himself that the provision proposed is a proper provision in view of the nature of the emergency.

A provincial legislature may continue to exercise its legislative functions despite the proclamation of a state of emergency. If, however, any provision of a Provincial law is repugnant to any provision of a Federal law which the Federal Legislature has power to make during the continuance of the emergency, the Federal law, whether passed before or after the Provincial law, is to prevail, and the Provincial law to the extent of the repugnancy, but so long only as the federal law continues to have effect, is to be void.

**A Proclamation of Emergency—**

(a) may be revoked by a subsequent proclamation;

(b) is to be communicated forthwith to the Secretary of State and laid by him before each House of Parliament; and

(c) is to cease to operate at the expiration of six months, unless before the expiration of that period it has been approved by Resolution of both Houses of Parliament.

A law made by the federal legislature which that legislature would not but for the issue of a proclamation of Emergency have been competent to make is to cease to have effect on the expiration of a period of six months after the proclamation has ceased to operate, except as respects things done or omitted to be done before the expiration of that period.

## 2.9 RESTRICTION OF LEGISLATIVE POWERS

The act places a number of restrictions upon the exercise of legislative powers both by the federal legislature and by the provincil legislatures. These restrictions are set out in section 108 which provides as follows -

108 - (1) Unless the Governor-General in his discretion thinks fit to give his previous sanction, there shall not be introduced into, or moved in, either Chamber of the Federal Legislature, any Bill or amendment which -

(a) repeals, amends or is repugnant to any provisions of any act of Parliament extending to British India; or

(b) repeals, amends or is repugnant to any Governor-Genaral's or governor's Act, or any ordinance promulgated in his discretion by the Governor-General or a Governor; or

(c) affects matters as respects which the Governor-General is, by or under this Act, required to act in his discretion; or

(d) repeals, amends or affects any act relating to any police force; or

(e) affects the procedure for criminal proceedings in which European British subjects are concerned; or

(f) subjects persons not resident in British India to greater taxation than persons resident in British India or subjects companies not wholly controlled and managed in British India to greater taxation than companies wholly controlled and managed therein; or

(g) affects the grant of relief from any federal tax on income in respect of income taxed or taxable in the United Kingdom.

(2) Unless the Governor-General in his discretion thinks fit to give his previous sanction, there shall not be introduced into, or moved in, a Chamber of a Provincial Legislature any Bill or amendment which -

(a) repeals, amends or is repugnant to any provisions of any Act of Parliament extending to British India; or

(b) repeals, amends or is repugnant to any Governor-General's Act, or any ordinance promulgated in his discretion by the Governor-General; or

(c) affects matters as respects which the Governor-General is by or under this Act required to act in his discretion; or

(d) affects the procedure for criminal proceedings in which European British subjects are concerned;

and unless the Governor of the Province in his discretion thinks fit to give his previous sanction, there shall not be introduced or moved any Bill or amendment which -

(i) repeals, amends or is repugnant to any Governor's Act, or any ordinance promulgated in his discretion by the Governor; or

(ii) repeals, amends or affects any Act relating to any police force.

(3) Nothing in this section affects the operation of any other provision in this act which requires the previous sanction of the Governor-General or of a governor to the introduction of any bill or the moving of any amendment.

## 2.10.1 GOVERNOR-GENERAL'S ORDINANCES

Under the provisions of section 42 if at any time when the Federal Legislature is not in session the Governor-General is satisfied that circumstances exist which render it necessary for him to take immediate action, he may promulgate such ordinances as the circumstances appear to him to require. A proviso adds that the Governor-General -

(a) is to exercise his individual judgment as respects the promulgation of any ordinance under this section if a Bill containing the same provisions would, under the Act, have required his previous sanction to its introduction into the Legislature; and

(b) is not, without instructions from His Majesty, to promulgate any such ordinance if he would have deemed it necessary to reserve a bill containing the same provisions for the signification of His Majesty's pleasure.

An ordinance promulgated under this section is to have the same force and effect as an Act of the Federal Legislature assented to by this Governor-General, but every such ordinance -

(a) is to be laid before the Federal Legislature and is to cease to operate at the expiration of six weeks from the re-assembly of the legislature, or, if before the expiration of that period resolutions disapproving it are passed by both Chambers, upon the passing of the second of those resolutions;

(b) may be disallowed by the Crown;

(c) may be withdrawn at any time by the Governor-General.

If and so far as any such ordinance makes any provision which the Federal Legislature would be incompetent to enact, it is to be void.

It will be observed that the Governor-General can only exercise his powers under section 42 when the Federal Legislature is not in session. Section 43, however, empowers the Governor-General at any time to promulgate ordinances if he is satisfied that circumstances exist which render it necessary for him to take immediate action for the purpose of enabling him satisfactorily to discharge his functions in so far as he is required to act in his discretion or to exercise his individual judgment. An ordinance promulgated under section 43 is to continue in operation for such period, not exceeding six months, as may be specified therein, but may, by a subsequent ordinance, be extended for a further period not exceeding six months. It is to have the same force and effect as an act of the Federal Legislature but -

(a) may be disallowed by the Crown;

(b) may be withdrawn at any time by the Governor-General; and

(c) if it is an ordinance extending a previous ordinance for a further period, is to be communicated immediately to the Secretary of State and laid by him before each House of Parliament.

If at any time it appears to the Governor-General that for the purpose of enabling him satisfactorily to discharge his functions in so far as he is required to act in his discretion or to exercise his individual judgment, it is essential that provision should be made by legislation, he may by message to both chambers of the Legislature explain the circumstances which in his opinion render legislation essential and either -

(a) enact forthwith, as a Governor-General's Act, a Bill containing such provisions as he considers necessary; or

(b) attach to his message a draft of the Bill which he considers necessary.

Where the Governor-General attaches a draft to his message, he may at any time after the expiration of one month enact, as a Governor-General's Act, the Bill proposed by him to the chambers either in the form of the draft communicated to them or with such amendments as he meeds necessary; but before so doing he is to consider any address which may have been presented to him by either Chamber with reference to the Bill or to any suggested amendments. A Governor-General's Act is to have the same force and effect as an Act of the Federal Legislature. It may be disallowed by the Crown.

Every Governor-General's Act is to be communicated to the Secretary of State and laid by him before each House of Parliament.

## 2.10.2 FAILURE OF CONSTITUTIONAL MACHINERY

The Act contains special provisions enabling the Governor-General to act promptly in the event of a breakdown of the constitutional machinery. Under section 45, if at any time the Governor-General is satisfied that a situation has arisen in which the government of the Federation cannot be carried on in accordance with the provisions of the Act, he may, by Proclamation -

(a) declare that his functions shall to such extent as may be specified in the Proclamation be exercised by him in his discretion;

(b) assume to himself all or any of the powers vested in or exercisable by any Federal body or authority.

A Proclamation for these purposes may contain such incidental and consequential provisions as may appear to the Governor-General to be necessary or desirable for giving effect to it, including provisions for suspending in whole or in part the operation of any provisions of the Constitution relating to any Federal body. The Governor-General, however, is not enabled to assume to himself any of the powers vested in or exercisable by the Federal Court or to suspend, either in whole or, in part, the operation of any provision of the Act relating to that Court. One Proclamation may be revoked or varied by another.

When such a Proclamation is issued -

(a) it must be communicated to the secretary of State and laid by him before each House of Parliament; and

(b) unless it is a Proclamation revoking a previous Proclamation, it is to cease to operate at the expiration of six months.

It is provided, however, that, if and so often as a resolution approving the continuance in force of such a Proclamation is passed by both Houses of Parliament, the Proclamation, unless revoked, is to continue in force for a further period of twelve months from the date on which it would otherwise have ceased to operate. If at any time the government of the Federation has for a continuous period of three years been carried on under such a Proclamation, then, at the expiration of such period, the Proclamation is to cease to have effect and the government of the Federation is to be carried on in accordance with the provisions of the Act, subject to any amendment of it which Parliament may deem it necessary to make. If the Governor-General, by a Proclamation under section 45, assumes to himself any power of the Federal Legislature to make laws, any law made by him in the exercise of that power is to continue to have effect notwithstanding the revocation or expiration of the Proclamation.

It is interesting to compare these provisions with those contained in the Emergency Powers Act 1920 (10 & 11 Geo. V., c.55) which applies to the United Kingdom, and enables the Executive to rule by regulation after a Proclamation of emergency has been made. This power is, however, subject to a stricter because more immediate Parliamentary control.

## 2.10.3 GOVERNOR'S ORDINANCES

All Governors are to have powers, similar to those possessed by the Governor-General, to promulgate ordinances during recesses of the Provincial Legislature and, at any time, with respect to certain subjects. In addition, they are empowered to enact Acts in circumstances identical with those under which the Governor-General can exercise the same function in relation to the Federal Legislature. Section 93 provides that governors may issue Proclamations in the event of failure of constitutional machinery on practically the same terms as the Governor-General. The concurrence of the latter, however, must be obtained before such a proclamation can be made by a Governor."

(Reference : India's New Constitution - A Survey of the Government of India Act 1935 by J.P.Eddy and F.H.Lawton published by Macmillan And Co.,Ltd., St. Martin's Street, London 1935)

**2.11.1** As H.M. Seervai states in his book 3rd Edition, Volume II, Constitution of India, p. 2620, that "Venkatarama Aiyar J. rightly observed in M.P. V. Sundararamaier v. A.P. (1958) S.C.R.1422) that :

.... our Constitution was not written on a *tabula rasa*, that a Federal Constitution had been established under the Government of India Act, 1935, and though that had undergone considerable changes by way of repeal, modification and addition, it still remains the framework on which the present Constitution is built, and that the provisions of the Constitution must accordingly be read in the light of the provisions of the Government of India Act."

**29.12** Section 45 of the G.I., Act, 1935 provided for failure of constitutional machinery for the Federation in Part II, Chapter V of the Act entitled "Provisions in case of failure of constitutional machinery" and s. 93 provided for such failure in the Provinces in Part II, Chapter VI which was similarly entitled. Section 45(1) ran as follows :

"45 Power of Governor-General to issue Proclamations - (1) If at any time the Governor-General is satisfied that a situation has arisen in which the government of the Federation can not be carried on in accordance with the provisions of this act, he may by Proclamation -

(a) declare that his functions shall to such extent as may be specified in the Proclamation be exercised by him in his discretion;

(b) assume to himself all or any of the powers vested in or exercisable by any Federal body or authority.

and any such Proclamation may contain such incidental and consequential provisions as may appear to him to be necessary or desirable for giving effect to the objects of the Proclamation, including provisions for suspending in whole or in part the operation of any provisions of this Act relating to any Federal body or authority;

Provided that nothing in this sub-section shall authorise the Governor-General to assume to himself any of the powers vested in or exercisable by the Federal Court or to suspend, either in whole or in part, the operation of any provision of this Act relating to the Federal Court."

Section 93 was mutatis mutandis the same except that the Governors of Provinces were substituted for the Governor-General, and the Government of the Province was substituted for the Government of the Federation."

**2.11.2** While briefing the reasons for enacting Sections 45 and 93 of Government of India, 1935, Shri Seervai states that since there was the demand for self government at the provinces, it is necessary the Centre i.e. Federal Government must have such powers; secondly, to read Sections 12(1) (a) of Government of India Act, 1935 in conjunction with Section 102 of Government of India Act, 1935 the Governor-General shall have the following special responsibilities - the prevention of any grave menace to the peace or tranquillity of India or any part thereof. Further to add, in the House of Lords as Shri Seervai quoted "the Marquess of Lothian moved an amendment to add the following words to para 12(1) (a) - "or the subversion of the Institutions set up in this act."

"In moving this amendment the Marquess observed that by general consent the basis of the Bill was that it was intended to set up institutions based on responsible government in India. To secure this the Governor-General should be armed with adequate powers to intervene in the event of any attempt being made, while acting within constitutional forms, to subvert the principles of responsible government and substitute for them some form of party dictatorship. The proposed amendment was, however, withdrawn on an assurance given by the Marquess of Zetland that if a really serious attempt was made to subvert the Constitution, even by constitutional means it would be contrary to the general scheme set out in the Act and the Governor-General would be justified in taking action under section 45."

Section 72 of Government of India Act, 1919, states "The Governor-General may in cases of emergency make and promulgate ordinances for peace and good government of British India or any part thereof, and any ordinance so made shall for the space of not more than six months from its promulgation, have the like force of law as an Act passed by the Indian legislature; out the power of making ordinance under this section is subject to the like restrictions, as the power of the Indian legislature to make laws; and any ordinance made under this section is subject to the like disallowance as an Act passed by the Indian legislature and may be controlled or superseded by any such Act.

(Reference:AIR 1931 Privy Council 111 dt.27.2.1931 - Shri Bhagat Singh and Ors v Emperor).

**2.12.1** Prior to 1919 Act, it has been the practice for the British Empire to enter into treaties to protect any Indian State for its survival and to bring peace and tranquillity. This is evident in the case of Nabab of the Carnatic v East India Company (1792, 2 Ves. 60). Further, as early as 1773, the East India Company was in a position to obtain the signature of the

Ruler of Cooch Behar to a treaty of obedience and submissions. Similarly it is also found in the treaties of protection which were made with Mysore in 1799, Nagpur in 1860 and Bikaner in 1818. Further to add, the treaties of subordinate cooperation were signed both with Udaipur and Jotpur in 1818. To quote in the words of Eddy and Lawton, "The validity of the treaties and engagements made with the princes and the maintenance of their rights, privileges and dignities have been asserted and observed by the Paramount power. But the Paramount Power has had of necessity to make decision and exercise functions beyond the terms of treaties, in order to secure the observance of treaty obligations and the maintenance of the peace of India as a whole.

Rajasthan Vs. Union of India S.R.Bommai Vs. Union of India, Bhagat Singh Vs. Emperor of State Hill v. Brigg Mostyn v. FabrigasMusgrove v PulidoR.v.EyreM.P. V.Sundararamaier v. A.P. Nabab of the Carnatic v East India Company and the case of Hyderabad may be cited by way of illustration. In 1800 the British made a treaty with His Highness the Nizam, article 15 of contains the following clause -

"The Honourable Company's Government on their part hereby declare that they have no manner of concern with which any of His Highness children, relations, subjects, or servants, with respect to whom His Highness is absolute."

Yet as soon as 1804 the Indian Government successfully pressed the appointment of an individual as Chief Minister. In 1815 the same Government had to interfere because the Nizam's sons offered violent resistance to his orders. The administration of the State gradually sank into chaos. Cultivation fell off, famine prices prevailed, justice was not obtainable and the population began to migrate. The Indian Government was compelled again to intervene and in 1820 British officers were appointed to supervise the district administration with a view to protecting the cultivating classes. Later on again the Court of Directors instructed the Indian Government to intimate to the Nizam through the Residency that they could not remain "indifferent spectators of the disorder and misrule", and that unless there was improvement it would be the duty of the Indian Government to urge on His Highness the necessity of changing his minister and taking other measures necessary to secure good government." pp. 16 & 17.

In the Baroda case (1873 to 1875) the Crown as Paramount Power, found it necessary to define its authority and right to intervene where it is essential. In this connection, it is to note that a commission had been appointed to investigate complaints which were brought against the Gaekwar's Administration. This was protested by the Ruler and in reply to the protest, the viceroy and Governor-General Lord Northbrook, wrote -

"This intervention, although amply justified by the language of treaties, rests also on other foundations. Your Highness has justly observed that the British Government is undoubtedly the Paramount Power in India, and the existence and prosperity of the Native States depend upon its fostering favour and benign protection". (p.18 of India's New Constitution)".

Therefore, it is found that it has been the Paramount Power which is having total power to protect and to achieve peace and tranquillity of Nation States (Provinces). In the cases of Secretary of State for India in Council V Kamachee Boye Sahaba (1859) 13 Moo. P.C.C.22 and Salaman v Secretary of State for India in Council, 1906 1.K.B.1630, it is established that "Acts done by the Paramount Power in the Exercise of its authority in relation to the States or Acts of State which are not cognisable by any Court in either British India or in Great Britain." (p.22).

## 2.13.1 CONSTITUENT ASSEMBLY DEBATES - DRAFT CONSTITUTION OF INDIA

Articles 277 and 278 appeared in Part 13 of Draft Constitution entitled Emergency Provisions. The draft constitution of India was prepared by the Drafting Committee and published under the authority of Constituent Assembly in 1948. (H.M.Seervai 11 f.n. p.2622) This was submitted to the President of the Constituent Assembly of India by Dr. Ambedkar and in the covering letter dated 21.2.1948, Dr. Ambedkar wrote, "In preparing the Draft, the Drafting Committee was of course expected to follow the decisions taken by the Constituent Assembly or by the various Committees appointed by the Constituent Assembly. This the Drafting Committee has endeavored to do as far as possible. There were, however, some matters in respect of which the Drafting Committee felt it necessary to suggest certain changes. All such changes have been indicated in the draft by underlining the relevant portions. Care has also been taken by the drafting committee to insert a foot note explaining the reasons for every such change." ibid 2622.

**2.13.2** Dr.Ambedkar introduced a new draft article 277 (A) as follows :-

"It shall be the duty of the Union to protect every State against external aggression and internal disturbance and to ensure that the Government of every State is carried on in accordance with the provisions of this .Constitution".

Shri Seervai quotes in his foot note 15 it p.2623 that "from the revised article 278 was omitted the requirement in the earlier draft that there should, in addition, be a threat to the peace and tranquillity of a State". According to the revised article 278, the President could intervene in the affairs of a state, if, on a report of a Governor or otherwise, he was satisfied that a situation had arisen in which the Government of the State could not be carried on in accordance with the Provisions of the Constitution. On being so satisfied, the President can by a proclamation assume to himself the functions of the State Government or any State Authority. The revised draft article 278 is now article 356 and the new draft article 277 (A) 'is presently article 355. While initiating, the draft article 278, in the Constituent Assembly, Dr.Ambedkar said, "Now I come to the remarks made by my friend Pandit Kunzru. The first point, if I remember correctly, which was raised by him was that the power to take over the administration when the constitutional machinery fails is a new thing, which is not to be found in any constitution. I beg to differ from him and I would like to draw his attention to the article contained in the American constitution, where the duty of the United States is definitely expressed to be to maintain the republican for form of the constitution."

Further, Mr. Seervai quotes the words of Dr.Ambedkar as "I hope the first thing (the President) will do would be to issue a mere warning to a province that has erred that things were not happening in the way in which they were intended to happen in the constitution. If that warning fails, the second thing for him to do will be to order an election allowing the people ...... to settle matters by themselves. It is only when these two remedies failed that he would resort to this article."

**2.13.3** Mr.Seervai while analysing above speech of Dr.Ambedkar, he has made the following observations :-

(1) The article 278 (article 356 now) was meant to be a last resort.

(2) The President would issue warning which is important because such a warning serves a number of purposes like :

(a) the union government to specify where is the actual deviation or failure to carry on according to the provisions of the constitution by a State or States;

(b) on receipt of such warning, the state government is bound to either accept the charge or reject the charge with the suitable explanation;

(c) the arbitrary use of this article can be reduced/ eliminated.

(3) Before resorting to President Rule, the State Government machinery and the people of the State are given a chance to review the policies of the existing State Government.

(4) It has emphasised that the Parliament Government is a part of Federal Constitution in which the States will

have their own rights for which the Union has to enforce.

**2.13.4** Mr.Seervai while discussing the crucial element of the Presidential power to impose the president's rule to secure good government in the State and in this reference he narrates the following dialogue in the Constituent Assembly and the same is as follows :-

"Pandit Hirday Nath Kunzru (United Provinces: General) :- "May I ask my honourable Friend to make one point clear? Is it the purpose of article 278 and 278-A to enable the Central Government to intervene in provincial affairs for the sake of good government of the Provinces?"

The Honourable Dr.B.R.Ambedkar: "No, no. The Centre is not given that authority."

Pandit Hirday Nath Kunzru: "Or only when there is such misgovernment in the province as to endanger the public peace?"

The Honourable Dr. B.R.Ambedkar: "Only when the government is not carried on in consonance with the provisions laid down for the constitutional government of the provinces. Whether there is good government or not in the province is not for the Centre to determine. I am quite clear on the point."

As to the meaning of the words "according to the provisions of the Constitution" the following question and answer are important:

Pandit Hirday Nath Kunzru: "What is the meaning exactly of the provisions of the constitution taken as a whole? The House is entitled to know from the honourable member what is his idea of the meaning of the phrase in accordance with the provisions of the constitution."

The Honourable Dr.B.R.Ambedkar: "It would take me very long now to go into a detailed examination of the whole thing, and, referring to each article, say, this is the principle which is established in it and say, if any government or any legislature of a province does not act in accordance with it, that would act as a failure of machinery. The expression "failure of machinery", I find, has been used in the Government of India Act, 1935. Everybody must be quite familiar therefore with its *de facto* and *de jure* meaning. I do not think any further explanation is necessary."

It will be appropriate to refer here the words of Shri Seervai at p.2625, "It will be seen that the words we have italicized in Dr.Ambedkar's answer are an evasion of the difficulties pointed out by Pandit Kunzru. A heavy price has to be paid for this evasion in the years to come." Therefore, keeping in view of these words let us analyse article 356 in the next chapter.

# 3

# *Article 356: A Survey*

**3.1.1** Failure of Constitutional machinery in States - President's Rule in States is discussed in article 356. The other related provisions are found in articles 355, 357 and 365.

In addition to them, there are other related provisions which are pertaining to the powers and constitutional positions of the President and Governors.

**3.1.2** Article 355 states:

"Duty of the Union to protect states against external aggression and internal disturbance - it shall be the duty of the Union to protect every state against external aggression and internal disturbance and to ensure that the Government of every State is carried on in accordance with the principles of the constitution."

**3.1.3** Therefore, according to article 355 it can be construed that it is the duty of Union to ensure the state government to carry on in accordance with the provisions of the constitution when there is external aggression or internal disturbance.

Thus, the union shall interfere to protect the govt. of every state under two circumstances namely

(1) External aggression; and
(2) Internal disturbance,

by which there could be every likelihood of destabilisation caused to the government of every state or any state. In other words, but for above mentioned two circumstances the union govt. would not interfere in the internal affairs of the govt. of every state or any state and moreover, the federal structure would not be altered. During the President's rule, the federal structure is altered as reflected in articles 357 and 365. This includes the article 356 also in addition to article 353 in reference to proclamation of National emergency under article 352. In addition to above, this is also evident during the financial emergency proclamation.

**3.2.1** Section 51 of the Part V of the Common Wealth of Australia Constitution Act, 1900, reads :-

"Section 51 - Legislative Powers of the Parliament - the parliament shall, subject to this constitution have power to make laws for the peace, order and good government of the Common wealth with respect to :- ..........."

There are 39 items under this section in order to achieve peace, order and good government of Commonwealth. Similarly, there is the section 52 which deals with the exclusive powers of the Parliament and section 52 reads as follows :-

"Exclusive powers of the Parliament:- the parliament, shall, subject to this constitution, have power to make laws for the peace, order and good government of the Commonwealth ......"

This section applies to three areas. Thus, both sections 51 and 52 do provide powers to Parliament (Commonwealth of Australia) to make laws for the purpose of and maintenance of peace, order and good government of the Commonwealth in 42 specific areas.

Hence, it shows that it is the responsibility of the Commonwealth of Australia to achieve peace, order and good government.

Further under section 51(6), reading with section 102, the Parliament has powers to make laws for the government of any territory. Similarly, by Section 119, it is the duty of the Commonwealth to protect "every state against invasion and on the application of the executive government of the state against domestic violence". (p.473 of Australian constitution by Colin Howard, 3rd edition, the Law Book Co.Ltd.,1985). This is falling under the defence power of federal government.

**3.2.2** Section 119 of Chapter V - The States of Commonwealth of Australia, Constitution Act, 1900, reads as follows :-

"Protection of State from invasion and violence. - - The Commonwealth shall protect every state against invasion and on the application of executive government of the state, against the domestic violence".

Hence, the parliament has power to make the laws for peace, order and good government of Commonwealth and there is also the duty of Commonwealth to protect the states from invasion and violence.

In the case of Adelaide Company of Jehovah's witnesses Incorporated V Commonwealth (1943) 67 C.L.R. 116 (H.C) Williams J. held,

"...... It is the duty of the Commonwealth under section 119 of the constitution to protect every' state against the invasion. This duty must by fulfilled in order to preserve the constitutions of the states and the rights of citizens and corporations and the laws of the states." (p.509 Cases on the constitution of the Commonwealth of Australia by Geoffery Sawer LL.M.,Australia, The Law Book Co. of Australasion PTY Ltd. 1948.

Isaacs J, held, "...... by Section 119 the Commonwealth is commanded to protect every state against invasion" in the case of Faray Vs Burvett (1916) 21 C.L.R. 433 (H.C).p.240 of the cases on the Constitution of the Commonwealth of Australia, Geofferey Sawer LL.M.

**3.3.1** In Canada, Section 91 reads as follows :-

"Section 91 - it shall be the lawful duty for the Queen, by and with the advice and consent of the Senate and House of Commons, to make laws for peace, order and good government of Canada ...."

Section 91 is conferring the residuary nature of power on the federal power of Canada. Invoking the emergency power under section 91 the Emergency Power Act, 1950-51 was passed during the Korean War. The Energy Supplies Emergency Act, 1973-74 was enacted after the 1973 Yom Kippur war when there was a threat of an oil shortage.

There is one important limitation on the federal emergency power that it will support only temporary measures. p.226 of constitutional Law of Canada, Peter W. Hogg, The Carswell Co.Ltd., Tornonto, Canada, 1977.

**3.3.2** Bora Laskin narrates the historical interpretation of the founding fathers on section 91, and states,

"In support of this general position they place importance on the opening paragraph of Section 91 which have dominion power to make laws for the peace, order, and good Government of Canada," in relation to all matters not exclusively assigned to the provincial legislatives. This phrase had acquired a wide, though not very precise, significance in the legislative history of the British Empire before 1867. "Peace, Order and Good Government" and the variation, , "Peace, Welfare and Good Government" where the phrases habitually used by the British colonial authorities in wasting Colonial legislatures with the full range of legislative powers." (p. 7 of Canadian Constitutional Law, The Carswall Company Ltd.,Canada 1951).

**3.4.1** Article 356 which has incorporated the provisions of the constitution on this account, reads as follows :-

356 (1) If the President, on receipt of a report from the governor of a state or otherwise is satisfied that a situation has arisen in which the government of the state can not be carried on in accordance with the provisions of this constitution, the President may by proclamation -

(a) assume to himself all or any of the functions of the government of the state and all or any of the powers vested in or exercisable by the governor or any body or authority in the state other than the legislature of the state;

(b) declare that the powers of the legislature of the state shall be exercisable by or under the authority of Parliament;

(c) make such incidental and consequential provisions as appear to the President to be necessary or desirable for giving effect to the objects of the proclamation, including provisions for suspending in whole or in part the operation of any provisions of this constitution relating to any body or authority in the state;

Provided that nothing in this clause shall authorise the President to assume to himself any of the powers rested in or exercisable by a high court, or to suspend in whole or in part the operation of any provision of this constitution relating to high courts.

(2) Any such proclamation may be revoked or varied by a subsequent proclamation.

(3) Every proclamation under this article shall be laid before each House of Parliament and shall except where it is a proclamation revoking a previous proclamation, cease to operate at the expiration of two months unless before the expiration of that period it has been approved by resolutions of both the Houses of Parliament:

Provided that if any such proclamation (not being a proclamation revoking a proclamation) is issued at a time when the House of the People is dissolved or the dissolution of the House of the People takes place during the period of two months referred to in this clause, and if a resolution approving the proclamations has been passed by the Council of States, but no resolution with respect to such proclamation has been passed by the House of the People before the expiration of that period, the proclamation shall cease to operate at the expiration of thirty days from the date on which the House of the People first sits after its reconstitution unless before the expiration of the said period of thirty days a resolution approving the proclamation has been also passed by the House of the People.

(4) A proclamation so approved shall, unless revoked, cease to operate on the expiration of a period of six months from the date of issue of the Proclamation:

Provided that if and so often as a resolution approving the continuance in force of such a proclamation is passed by both Houses of Parliament, the proclamation shall, unless revoked, continue in force for a further period of six months from the date on which under this clause it would otherwise have ceased to operate, but no such proclamation shall in any case remain in force for more than three years:

Provided further that if the dissolution of the House of the People takes place during any such period of six months and a resolution approving the continuance in force of such proclamation has been passed by the Council of States, but no resolution with respect to the continuance in force of such proclamation has been passed by the House of the People during the said period, the proclamation shall cease to operate at the expiration of thirty days from the date on which the House of the People first sits after its reconstitution unless before the expiration of said period of thirty days a resolution approving the continuance in force of the proclamation has been also passed by the House of the People.

(Provided also that in the case of proclamation received under clause (1) on the eleventh day of May, 1987 with respect to the State of Punjab, the reference in the first proviso to this clause to "3 years" shall be construed as a reference to (five years).)

(5) Notwithstanding anything contained in clause (4) a resolution with respect to the continuance in force of a

proclamation approved under clause (3) for any period beyond the expiration of one year from the date of issue of such proclamation shall not be passed by either House of Parliament unless -

(a) a proclamation of emergency is in operation, the whole of India or, as the case may be, in the whole or in any part of the state, at the time of the passing of such resolution, and

(b) the Election Commission certifies that the continuance in force of the proclamation approved under clause (3) during the period specified in such resolution is necessary on account of difficulties in holding general elections to the legislative assembly of the State concerned.

(Provided that nothing in this clause shall apply to the proclamation issued under clause (1) on the eleventh day of May, 1987 with respect to the state of Punjab).

**3.4.2** Article 365 states when there is a failure of the constitutional machinery in a state. Article 365 reads as follows :-

"Effect of failure to comply with, or to give effect to, directions given by the Union. - Where any state has failed comply with, or to give effect to, any directions given in the exercise of the Executive Power of the Union under any of the provision of this constitution, it shall be lawful for the President to hold that a situation has arisen in which the government of the state can not be carried on in accordance with the provision of this constitution."

Therefore, the constitution provides clearly that when there it could be construed that there is a failure of constitutional machinery in a state. This is made very clear under Article 365.

Once the President rule is imposed under article 356, the following changes are taken place :-

**3.4.3** "Article 357. - Exercise of legislative powers under Proclamation issued under article 356. -

(1) where by a proclamation issued under clause (1) of article 356, it has been declared that the powers of the legislature of the state shall be exercisable by or under the authority of Parliament, it shall be competent -

(a) for Parliament to confer on the President the power of the legislature of the state to make laws, and to authorise the President to delicate, subject to such conditions as he may think fit to impose, the power so conferred to any other authority to be specified by him in that behalf;

(b) for Parliament or for the President or other authority in whom such power to make laws is vested under sub clause (a) to made laws conferring powers and imposing duties, or authorising the conferring of powers and the imposition of duties upon the union or offices and authorities thereof;

(c) for the President to authority when the House of the People is not in session expenditure from the consolidated fund of the state pending the sanction of such expenditure by Parliament.

(2) Any law made in exercise of the power of the legislature of the state by Parliament or the President or other authority referred to in sub clause (a) of clause (1) which Parliament or the President or such other authority would not but for the issue of a proclamation under article 356, have been competent to make, shall, after the Proclamation has ceased to operate, continue in force until altered or repealed or amended by a competent legislature or other authority.

**3.5.1** Till date there have been 83 occasions when the President's rules has been imposed under article 356. The latest one is the dissolution of 3 legislative assemblies namely

(1) State of Himachal Pradesh

(2) State of Madhya Pradesh; and

(3) State of Uttar Pradesh.

the imposition of President's rule under article 356 was in the wake of December 6, 1992, Ayodhya Issue. The affected Patwa government filed a case in the M.P.High Court challenging the proclamation order of President under article 356 and in pursuant to it the MP High Court reversed the proclamation order of President's rule under article 356 and ordered to reconstitute the dissolved assemblies. Within the permitted period the Union Government filed in the Supreme Court against the order/judgement of MP High Court and the Supreme Court of India has had stayed the order of the MP High Court. Since the case is still subjudice nothing would be offered at this moment except the fact that the MP High Court could reverse the proclamation order of President's rule under article 356 stating the subjective satisfaction of the President of India is subject to judicial review. But, however, it is blatantly found the abuse of this power by resorting to the imposition of President's rule under article 356 in Tamilnadu. This is made clear in the words of Prof.T.K.Tope, "Naked abuse of power under article 356 by the Government of India was once again exhibited in 1990. In the State of Tamilnadu, there was a ministry headed by Shri M.Karunanidhi who was the leader of the DMK Party. He commanded majority in the House and there was no constitutional crisis of any kind in the State. The President of India, Shri R.Venkataraman, on the advice of Prime Minister, Shri Chandra Shekhar, who headed a minority government with only 56 members of his party in Lok Sabha, issued a proclamation under article 356 and dismissed the Karunanidhi Ministry and dissolved the legislative assembly. The Chandra Shekhar Government would continue in office because of the support of the Congress Party headed by Shri Rajiv Gandhi in Lok Sabha. It must be noted that the Governor of Tamilnadu, Shri Barnala, had not sent any report to the President as regards failure of constitutional machinery in the state. The governor made a public statement to that effect. Even then, the President dismissed the ministry and dissolved the assembly. It must be stated that the President

Venkataraman had the recommendations of Sarkaria Commission before him. Moreover, he should have at least asked Prime Minister, Shri Chandra Shekhar to reconsider the advise. But he did not do so. This was an unfortunate act on the part of the Union Government. Recently the recommendation of the Cabinet was returned back for reconsideration of the Cabinet by the President Shri K. R. Narayanan on the imposition of President's rule under Article 356 in UP. Similarly recommendation of HP's Governor to the Union Govt was returned back for reconsideration.

**3.5.2** Article 356 may be relied upon by the Union Government in order to appoint commissions of inquiry into the conduct of the chief ministers and other ministers, with a view to ensure that the administration in the state is carried on in accordance with the provisions of the constitution. However, abuse of this power for political purposes can not be ruled out. Actually, this power had been abused both by the Congress government as well as by the Janta government. No doubt, it is true that appointment of such commissions is an encroachment on the autonomy of states but such appointments have been held to be valid. "pp.855 to 856, Constitutional Law of India, 2nd edition, Eastern Book Company, 1992.

Further, Prof.Tope has made this observation as found in his words, "invocation of article 356 in Kerala in 1959 was an instance abuse of the power conferred upon by the article on the Government of India. "ibid 858.

**3.5.3** According to article 356, the President can act on the report of the Governor of the State or even otherwise, which means that the President shall receive information from some other source about the failure of the constitutional machinery in the state and might take action on that information only. But in the case of 1990, President's Rule in the state of Tamilnadu imposed by resorting to the clause " or even otherwise". This is the first time resorted to in the Constituent

Assembly debate, as stated by Prof.Tope that Allady Krishnaswamy Aiyer explained that the term President meant the Union Government. In other words, the Council of Minsters of the Union Cabinet shall make recommendation to the President of India for imposing President's rule under article 356. Whereas, in the case of 1990, the minority government of Chandra Shekhar had not had the total representation of people of India since the number of members of Chandra Shekhar Government were only 56 out of 525. Therefore, even the minority government which has not enjoyed the majority views of the people or the members of the Parliament could resort to invoke article 356 on the recommendation to the President of India is absolutely a blatant abuse of power given under article 356. This view may be an extreme proposition, which needs impartial analysis.

**3.5.4** The consequences of imposition of President's rule in a state resulting to :

(1) the council of ministers in the state shall be dissolved and the President will assume to himself all or any of the function of the governor of the state.

(2) The legislature of the state may be dissolved and its power shall be exercisable by and under the authority of Parliament. Parliament may itself legislate for the state or authority the President to legislate.

This position above mentioned are made clear under article 357.

As per article 365, if there is a failure of constitutional machinery of a government, there should be a provision as stated in article 365 that the President of India on the recommendation of the Union Cabinet, in writing, shall proclaim the President's rule under article 356. When there is a failure of constitutional machinery, if such provision is not available then the democratic fibre of the nation will be lost. This is in the case of many instances where the President's rule stopped the misrule and had given opportunity to the people to elect their new representatives with different mandates. Further to add, this is on the basis of the recommendations received from the governor who is the representative of the Union Government and who also is the Head of the State of the state government and is having every opportunity to apprise the President of India about the peace, order and good government of the State which has not failed in the constitutional machinery.

**3.6.1** But, however, as highlighted above there have been more instances of abuse of power under article 356. In this connection, it will be appropriate to make mention of the recommendations of the Sarkaria Commission relating to emergency provision in the article 356. The recommendations are found in the words of Prof.Tope and are as follows :-

"(1) Article 356 should be used very sparingly. A warning should be issued to the errant state in specific terms before taking action under article 356. However, this would not be applicable to a situation when not taking immediate action would lead to disastrous consequences.

"(1) Article 356 should be used very sparingly

(2) The state legislative assembly should not be dissolved either by the Governor or the President before the proclamation under article 356 (1) has been laid before the Parliament and has had an opportunity to consider it. Article 356 should be suitably amended.

(3) Material facts and grounds on which article 356 (1) is invoked should be made an integral part of the proclamation issued. This should be achieved by a suitable amendment.

(4) In clause 5 of article 356 the word "and" occurring between sub clause (a) and (b) should be substituted by "or". p.857 ibid.

However, to note as a matter of interest that no COURT can issue a mandamus to compel the Union Government to impose President's rule in a state - D.Satyanarayan V N.T.Rama Rao, AIR 1988 AP 69.

# 4

# *Justiciability of a Presidential Proclamation*

Justiciability of a Presidential Proclamation under article 356 shall be analyzed in reference to the doctrine of political question and the scope for judicial review in the light of Rajasthan Assembly dissolution case.

## 4.1 DOCTRINE OF POLITICAL QUESTION AS A LIMITATION ON JUDICIAL REVIEW

Finkelstein in Judicial Self-limitation, 37 Harvward.L.Rev. 338, 344, (1924) held :

"There are certain cases which are completely without the sphere of judicial interference. They are called for historical reasons "Political Questions". The term applies to all those matters of the Court, at a given point of time, will be of the opinion that it is impolitic or inexpedient to take jurisdiction. Sometimes this idea of expediency will result from the fear of the vastness of the consequences that a decision on the merits might entail."

At the same time, a crucial view is seen from Frank, "Political Questions", in Supreme Court and Supreme Law 36, 46 (CAHN) edition 1954, " the basic objective of a plan of government are to be put the responsibility for the decision of questions some place, and the political question doctrine is usual when it operates to put responsibility at the best place, and is harmful when it puts the decision no place. What happens in the redistracting cases is that the responsibility, if not taken by the Court, is transferred to a body which has a completely *vested* interest in the mal- distracting."

**4.1.2** The political questions have been discussed in many cases in U.S.A. Baker v Carr (369, 'U.S. 186, 82 Supreme Court, 691, 7 L. 2nd edition, 663, 1962) discusses the political question and its justiciability. Mr. Justice Brennan held :

"the mere fact that the suit seeks protection of a political right does not mean it presents a political question. Such an objection "is little more than a play upon words" rather it is argued that *apportionment* cases, whatever the actual wording of the complaint, can involve no federal constitutional right except one resting on the guarantee of a republican form of government (article IV section 4) and that complaints based on the clause has been held to present political questions which are not justiciable.

We hold that the claim pleaded here neither rests upon nor implicates the guarantee clause and that its justiciability is therefore not foreclosed by our decision of cases involving that clause. Review of a number of political questions reveals that in the guarantee cases and in other political question cases it is the relationship between the judiciary and the coordinate branches of the federal government, and not the federal judiciary's relationship to the states, which give rise to the political question.

**4.1.3** The non-justiciability of a political question is primarily a function of separation of powers." While reviewing the cases Oetjen vs. Central Leather Company 246 US 297, 302, 38 SC 309, 311, 62 L.Ed.,726. and in this case it was held that "The conduct of the foreign relations of a government is committed by the constitution to the executive and legislative - the political - departments of the government, and the proprietary of what may be done in the exercise of this political power is not subject to judicial inquiry or decision." In the case of Baker vs. Carr, it is held in this connection, that "Yet it is error to suppose that every case is a controversy which touches foreign relations, lies beyond judicial cognizance." Further, Baker Vs. Carr case reviewed the case of Martin vs. Mott, 12 wheat, 19, 30, 6 L.ed. 537, and according to this case it is stated that though it has been stated broadly that the power which declared the necessity is the power to declare its cessation, and what the cessation request, hereto analysis reveals *isolable* reasons for the presence of political questions, underlying this court's refusal to review the political department's determination of when or whether war has ended. Dominant is the need for finality in the political determination for the where of emergency demands "a prompt and unhesitating obedience".

**4.1.4** Gardener vs Collector was also revealed in Baker's case. According to this case, it is held that the political question doctrine, a tool for maintenance of governmental order will not be so applied as to promote any disorder.

**4.1.5** In the Baker's case it is held after reviewing above cases that " unless one of these formulations is inextricable from the case at par, there should be no dismissal for non-justiciability on the ground of a political question presence."

**4.1.6** According to Guarantee Clause Article IV Section 4, it is held that "we shall discover that Guarantee Clause claims involved those elements which define a political question and for that reason and no other, they are not justiciable. In particular, we shall discover that the non-justiciability of such claims has nothing to do with their touching upon matters of state governmental organisation." Further, it is held in Baker's case "the doctrine of which we treat is one of "political questions" not one of "political cases". The courts can not reject as "no law suit" a bonafide controversy as to whether some action dominated "political" exceeds constitutional authority."

Article IV Section 4 of the U.S.Constitution deals here the Guarantee Clause and it reads : "That United States shall guarantee to every state in this union a republican form of government, and shall protect each of them against invasion; and on application of the legislature, or of the executive (when the legislature can not be convened) against domestic violence." The court found in the Baker's case that the guarantee clause cases involved the elements of a political question and thus are not justiciable. But since those reasons for non-justiciability have "nothing to do with their touching on matters of state governmental organisation" a re-apportionment case is not foreclosed from judicial review when it is based on a claim of denial of equal protection."

**4.1.7** In the recent case of United States vs. Nixon, 418 U.S. 683, 1974, the Court rejected the argument that a claim of executive privilege is a political question. In this connection, first case discussed political question doctrine was in 1849 and the court held that Guarantee Clause is not justiciable. Therefore, it is appropriate to quote the words of Rotunda, "the political question doctrine - which holds that certain matters are really political in nature and best resolved by the body politic rather than suitable for judicial review - is a misnomer.", p. 109, Constitutional Law, 2nd edition, Jain Paul, Minn, West publishing Company, 1983.

**4.1.8** Further to state in the words of Rotunda in Modern Constitutional Law, cases and notes, 2nd edition 1985, that, "Recalls that Chief Justice Marshall stated in Marbury vs. Madison: the province of the court is, solely to decide on the rights of the individual, not to inquire how the executive, or executive officers, perform duties in which they have a discretion. Questions in their nature political, or which are by the constitution and laws, submitted to the executive, can never be made in this court."

It is very interesting statement made by Rotunda while making consolidated opinions is the case of Baker vs Carr as "note that in Baker vs Carr the majority finds that there is an injury but that does not tell us what the remedy might be" ibid p. 52.

**4.1.9.1** On the political questions Baker vs. Carr has evolved this test as follows :-

"Prominent on the suffice of any case held to involve a political question is found a textually demonstrable constitutional commitment of the issue to a coordinate political department; or a lack of judicially discoverable and manageable standards for resolving it; or the impossibility of deciding without an initial policy determination of a kind clearly for non-judicial discretion; or the impossibility of a court's undertaking independent resolution without expressing lack of the respect due coordinate branches of government; or an unusual need for unquestioning adherence to a political decision already made; or the potentiality of embarrassment from multi-ferrous pronouncements by various departments on one question". p.110-111, Constitutional Law, John E.Nowak, Ronald D. Rotunda, J.Nelson Young, 1983 edition.

But however the court found that the Guarantee Cases involved the elements of a political question and thus are non justiciable. The guarantee clause is found in article IV section 4 of the United States Constitution which reads as follows :-

"The United States shall guarantee to every state in this union a Republican Form of Government, and shall protect each of them against invasion; and on application of the legislature, or of the Executive (when the Legislature can not be convened) against domestic violence."

Further, there were two more tastes known as Functional Taste evolved recently in addition to Baker Taste of political question and they are as follows :-

**4.1.9.2** Prof.Bickel has argued : "such is the foundation in both intellect and instinct, of the political question doctrine; the court's sense lack of capacity, compounded in unequal parts of (a) the strangeness of the issue and its interactibility to principled resolution; (b) the cheer momentousness of it, which tends to unbalanced judicial judgment; (c) the anxiety, not so much that the judicial judgment will be ignored as that perhaps it should but will not be; (d) finally, ("in a mature democracy"), the inner vulnerability, the self doubt of an institution which is electorally irresponsible and has no earth to draw strength from". A.Bickel, THE LEAST DANGEROUS BRANCH, 184, 1962, referred p. 118-119 of Constitutional Law, 1983.

**4.1.9.3** Another test is suggested by Prof.Henkin in his Book, Is There a "Political Question" Doctrine? 85, Law Journal, 597, 622-623, 1976. This is referred in the Constitutional Law p 119 ibid as follows :-

"Prof.Henkin has proposed another analysis;

the "Political Question"Doctrine, I conclude is an unnecessary, decepting packaging of several established doctrines.... I see its proper content as consisting of the following propositions:

(1) The courts are, bound to accept decisions by the political branches within their constitutional authority;

(2) the Courts will not find limitations or prohibitions on the powers of the political branches where the constitution does not prescribe any.

(3) Not all constitutional limitations or prohibitions imply rights and standing to object in favour of private parties.

(4) The courts may refuse some (or all) remedies for want of equity.

(5) In principle, finally, there might be constitutional provisions which can properly be interpreted as wholly or in part "Self-monitoring" and not the subject of judicial review. (but the only one the courts have found is the "Guarantee Clause" as applied to challenges to state action, and even that interpretation was not inevitable.")

**4.1.9.4** Further Prof.Rotunda in his Book makes the reference of Prof.Scharpf who has detailed analysis in his book, "Judicial Review at the Political Question: a functional analysis 75 Law Journal 1966". According to Prof.Scharpf the political question doctrine can be best explained in functional terms rather than an unprincipled retreat from difficult cases or the absence of applicable legal standards. He further states that the doctrine is justified when the court can not be assured of full clarification of the relevant questions because of difficulties of access to information. This is nothing but the repetition of Baker vs. Carr case. Prof.Scharpf explained the functional analysis in the following words :-

"This function is most obvious in the cases touching upon foreign relations where the court has generally been hesitant to trust its own understanding of the broader situation." Further, in the case of purely domestic issues he states, "for the decisions concerning the ratification of constitutional amendments , legislative enactments and the duration of the Civil War", the rationale of political question does not find convincing. Further, Prof.Scharpf states that the political question doctrine is explained in part as the court's deference to the prior decisions of another department within the latter's sphere of specific responsibility. In other words, allowing political question as non-justiciable is not due to lack of power of the court but because of understanding. However, this argument of Prof.Scharpf is found unfounding his exposition of political question doctrine.

**4.1.9.5** Dr.D.D.Basu has summed up the developments in view of judicial pronouncement in the Baker vs. Carr on the area of non-justiciability on political questions and has given summaries statement which could be made use of the Indian judiciary and they are as follows :-

"(i) The mere fact that a litigant seeks the protection of a political right does not mean that it presents a political question.

(ii) Whether a matter raises a political question, i.e.,

whether it has been committed by the constitution to another branch of government is itself a matter for judicial determination because the Constitution has made the Supreme Court the ultimate interpreter of the constitution.

(iii) The court having the responsibility to act as the ultimate interpreter of the constitution, is free to override the view taken on the relevant provision by another organ of the government, without being charged with confrontation with another co-ordinate department .

(iv) Even where a matter relates to a political right, such as the right to vote, the matter would be justiciable and the person aggrieved shall have a legal right to relief, if it is shown that the Bill of Rights has been violated by the State action relating thereto, e.g., the equal protection under the 14th Amendment. Hence, though the question of legislative apportionment under the Fourteenth Amendment (s.2) is of a legislative and, accordingly, of a political nature, the court will invalidate a State apportionment statute which violates the 'one man, one vote' principle which follows from the equal protection clause. Of course, the court would demand substantial equality and not 'mathematical' or 'absolute' equality, which would be an impossibility to attain.

(v) Even where an express provision of the constitution purports to exclude the jurisdiction of the court, e.g., Art.I, s.5(1) of the constitution, which says: "Each House shall be the judge of the elections, returns and qualifications of its own members" and Cl. (2) of that section empowers each House `to expel's member with the concurrence of two-thirds of its members, it would be within the jurisdiction of the court to interpret the true scope of these provisions of the constitution, regardless of what the legislature has assumed it to be, and give relief to a person who has been expelled in a case outside the true scope of such provisions, as interpreted by the Supreme Court.

In this case the court held that the only ground upon which the House of Representatives could refuse to admit a duly elected member was that he lacked the qualifications for membership, e.g., age, citizenship and residence, as contained in Art. I, s.1 (2) and not any general ground of unfitness, disreputable character or the like, and that the House could not rely on the power to 'expel' under Art.I, s.5(2), when the resolution of the House purported to 'exclude' and not to 'expel'.

Similarly, it has been held that the immunity to members of Congress "not to be questioned in any other place" "for any speech or debate in either House:, [Art.I,s.6(1)] is founded on the doctrine of Separation of Powers, or, in other words, judicial review has been excluded from this sphere on the ground that the Judiciary should not interfere with the activities of co-ordinate branch of the government, i.e., the Legislature, while it is exercising its legitimate functions. The legitimate functions of a Congressman are, however, confined to his `legitimate legislative activity and the object of the immunity is "to protect the integrity of the legislative process by insuring the independence of individual legislators". It follows, therefore, that the non-justiciability or exclusion of judicial review would not extent to any activity of a Congressman outside the proceedings of the House or its committees, related to speech or debate', e.g., employment or discharge of a employee by Congressman. Such discharge can, therefore, be challenged before a Court of law on the ground of violating of `due process' guaranteed by the fifth amendment. Similarly, publication by a member outside the House of his speech or other matters, would not be protected from the law of defamation.

(vi) In short, courts cannot reject a bona fide controversy as to whether some action denominated 'political' exceeds constitutional authority."

## 4.2 SCOPE FOR JUDICIAL REVIEW IN THE LIGHT OF RAJASTHAN ASSEMBLY DISSOLUTION CASE.

**4.2.1** Mauro Cappelletti in his Judicial Review in the Contemporary World, p 97-98, states "Judicial Review is a theme with many variations and subtle implications. The basic motive is a product of our common Western History;. the variations arrive inevitably from differences of experience and outlook within this larger framework. The subtleties, finally, centre about the ambiguous nature of judicial review in any democratic state.

The theme of modern constitutionlism is the embodiment of "natural law" principles in the positive law of the state. While classical antiquity and medieval Europe had at times affirmed the theoretical right of the citizen to disobey the unjust law, the right remained theory only. It was left to times nearer our own to seek an instrument to protect principles considered fundamental."

"....... The old World moved from legal to constitutional justice." Further he states, "The theoretical power of the judge of constitutionality is awesome; yet in the end he has "neither words nor purse" and must depend on others to give his decision meaning". But, however, his statement that 'the United States and those countries which have followed its example strive to this day to confine judicial review within the traditional judicial framework, carefully disguised." This particular statement probably looks ill-conceived since Prof.H.L.A.Hart while delivering a speech to the American audience on the American jurisprudence he made critical about the American judicial review which in fact has got deviated from the decision of Chief Justice Marshall in Mrbury Vs. Madison. This he made reference to the article of "Taking Rights Seriously" by Prof.Ronald Dwarkin, which was modified version of "Hard Cases" previously published. While making critical study on this Prof.Hart said that there is a great dilemma between "Nobel Dream" and "Nightmare" which in other words since the judicial review has taken a deviation attempting to interpret political questions and the judiciary has lost much of its judiciousness. When it is accepted that particular judicial review tends to become Nobel Dream otherwise it is mere Nightmare. In the continental judiciary system like Austrian eventhough initially there was a political review concept by the constitutional court but subsequently it has become like any other common law judicial review of Britain wherein there is a strict discipline in exercising judicial review without getting involved into the political decisions of the government. There he states that it may look the Common Law Concept which is most conservative and the American Concept of Judicial Review may glitter like dynamism in the Jurisprudence but this is nothing but Nightmare.

**4.2.2** John' Bell in his Book on Policy Arguments in Judicial Decisions published by Oxford at the Clarendon Press 1983, analyses the judicial function in contemporary Government. In the first chapter he discusses, "The political role of the judge and thereby he states "Traditionally, the view had been taken that judging is an activity which is very much apart from what is normally called "Politics". While few today would use the language of Montesquieu, describing the judges as "But the mouth which pronounces the words of the law", the distinction between judging and politics remains embedded in the common understanding of a legal system, certainly as it operates in most western countries ....- in the face of such an apparent divergence between the theory of the judicial function and actual practice, it would seem appropriate to consider how far the judicial role is indeed "political" and in what ways it may be understood as different from the activities of those whom we usually call "politicians". "p.1 ibid.

He further states, "......whereas during the Second World War and in the immediate post war period the judges were reluctant to interfere with the exercise of power by the Executive, since the 1960s a more critical attitude has been adopted and the judges are more willing to control and question the use of Executive power (reference:- R.Stevens, Judges and Politics (London, 1979); S.A.de Smith, Judicial Review of Administrative Action (4th ed. by J.M.Evans, London 1980)". The Executive is no longer the sole judge of the reasonableness of its use of power." However, this particular aspect of his view is not made clear how the changes take place. Since 1960s a more critical attitude has been adopted and the Judges are more willing to control and question the use of Executive power. Further, this argument has not made it clear to what extent the judges could get benefit out of it. However, he further states, "the cumulative effect of these developments has been to augment the power actually wielded by the judges and to increase their political importance. It becomes important to ask in what way these developments can be compatible with the view of the judge as a political neutral." But it is a fact that he makes a valuable comment in the following words :-

"In making new rules, in exercising discretionary powers, and in acting as a break to executive power, the judge can not help giving effect to distinctive political values, so that a claim that the judiciary is politically neutral would seem somewhat paradoxical." p.3 ibid

**4.2.3** On the adjudication he says " "Political" activity may best be described as an exercise of power giving direction to society. Where a decision maker has a choice of possible courses to take, his decision inevitably gives direction to society and he is engaging in politics in a deliberate way, rather than being involved in a political process in a passive, purely technical capacity. Such broad definition would certainly cover the activity of judges in some of the more difficult cases which confront them i.e., their value-choices, giving a certain direction to society. For example, in declaring administrative action to be unreasonable the judge is limiting the use of executive power to certain purposes which he considers to be within the range of reasonableness, and prevents it from being used to achieve other purposes which many politicians might feel are reasonable. The important questions which the holding of such political power raises are about the actual direction which will be given to society: whose values to be implemented, and are they right ones? It may be objected that this use of term is too broad in that it distorts the position in society which the judges occupy. The word "Political" it could be said, carries with it the connotation of partisanship which is inimical to the judicial function. However, since judges do have to make value-judgments in performance of their duties, they are, in the words of the French Cour de Cassation, `contribution to the creation of the State of the Law which will shape the society of tomorrow ". To ascertain and to describe the judicial' function as political in the sense outlined John Ball advocates three models such as :

(1) The consensus model;

(2) The rights model;

(3) The interstitial legislature model.

4.2.3.1 (1) **The Consensus model** :- This consensus model illustrates the interpretation of rules by the judge and in the words of John Ball, "I prefer therefore to use the word "interpret". This amounts to a claim that there is a qualitative, rather than simply a quantitative difference between the rule creating work of the court and that of the legislature. Such a claim can make sense of the view that the judge acts in a "neutral" way in making rules, whereas the legislatures and the Executive are more parties on."

**4.2.3.2 (2) The Rights Model** :- The Rights Model was proposed by Prof.R.Dwarkin, Dean and Prof. of jurisprudence, Oxford University, London. This concept first appeared as the hard case and subsequently it appeared in the name of taking right seriously. This particular revisioning of the hard cases was necessitated because of the criticisms from Prof.HAL Hart, Dr.Joseph Raz and other eminent jurists and in consequence he made it as a reply to the criticism and that has resulted in 'Taking Right Seriously' published in 1978. The rights model aims to enlarge the scope of judicial *acquamanship* to interpret and to create innovative interpretations between principles and policies. This point of view has been largely reflected in the recent judicial prònouncement both in U.S.A. and Britain. In USA this is vividly found in the case of Brown v Secondary

Board Education and in Britain Steel case. John Ball states "The justification which judges and legislatures can invoke are therefore different in kind, and different terms should be used to describe each. He proposes the term "principle" to characterize judicial reasons, which he asserts are only concerned with showing that a person has a right to the benefit he claims. On the other hand, policy should be used to characterize the legislative reasons which seek to show that a decision is in the interest of a community as a whole." p.15

**4.2.3.3 (3) The Interstitial Legislature Model :-** John Ball states, "The third model, which I shall call that of the 'interstitial legislature' consider that the task of the judge in hard cases are in applying vague, general standard is of fundamentally the same character as that of the legislature, though the former is subject to a number of constraints which do not affect the latter. Proponents of this model would argue that, where settled legal standards fail to produce an answer, the judge may be faced with a number of choices of rules or standards to resolve the case, each of which would not be wildly inconsistent with the existing law. In creating new rule in such circumstances, the judge has simply to exercise his own judgment on the suitability of the various options, and to decide what is best for the society as a whole. The standards of the legal system cannot dictate an answer to his problem, and, at best, they can only serve to narrow his options. This view, which was forcefully propounded by Geny, finds expression in art. I(2) of the 1907 Swiss Civil Code, which provides that, where the legal sources fail to provide an answer, the judge should decide the case `according to the rule which he would enact if he was legislator'. In other words, the judge has to exercise choice according to his personal views of what is in the collective interest, which is very similar to the way a legislator goes about making new rules."

**4.2.4** Based upon the above models, it was contended in many countries by the constitutional experts and jurists that the coercive power of the Centre should be regulated so that the power would not be abused. As Prof.De smith states, "Coercive powers may be *vested* in the Centre for use against a unit which seriously obstructs the working of the federal scheme of government. India furnishes the main precedent. If the executive power of a state is exercised so as not to secure due compliance with the law or so as to impede or prejudice the executive power of the Union, the central government may give any directions to the state that it considers necessary for the purpose of ending recalcitrance; and if the state fails to comply with a direction so given, the President may declare that the government of the state cannot be carried on in accordance with the constitution, whereupon full authority to carry on the government of the state *vests* in the Union "constitution articles 256, 257, 356, 357 and 365". The power of the Centre to remedy a breakdown on constitutional machinery in a state is also exercisable in other circumstances." p.275, The New Commonwealth and its Constitutions, London Slevens & Sons 1964.

**4.2.4.1** Therefore, the contention of judicial review on this extraordinary power of emergency has been subject to judicial scrutinisation whether the satisfaction of the executive to impose President's rule on the breakdown of constitutional machinery in a state has been subjected to. In 1931, the emergency power of Governor-General was challenged in reference to section 72 of Government of India Act, 1919. The Privy Council held and it is found in the words of Viscount Dupedin "A state of emergency that does not permit of any exact definition; it connotes a state of matters calling for drastic action which is to be judged as such by someone. It is more than obvious that someone must be Governor-General and be alone. Any other view would render utterly inert the whole provision. Emergency demands immediate action, and that action is prescribed to be taken by the Governor-General. It is he alone who can promulgate the ordinance." Further, with reference to the power of the Governor-General to promulgate the ordinance under section 72 it is further held, "The Governor-General is also the judge of that. The power given by section 72 is an absolute power, without any limits prescribed, except only that it can not do what the Indian legislatures would be unable to do, although it is made clear that it is only to be used in extreme cases of necessity where the good government of India demands it." It is also discussed whether the reasons to be given for resorting to that extreme power or otherwise. The answer is stated in his words, "Their Lordships must add that, although the Governor-General thought fit to expound the reasons which induced him to promulgate this ordinance, this was not in their Lordship's opinion in any way incumbent on him as a matter or law." The reference of this case is Bhagat Singh & Ors Vs Emperor 27.2.1931, AIR 1931 Privy Council 111, the Privy Council consisting of Viscount Dunedin, Lord Thankerton, Lord Russell of Killowen, St George Lowndes and SIR Dinshah Mulla.

**4.2.4.2.** The latest Privy Council's decision on this issue is Stephen Ķelong Ninghan V The Government of Malaysia, 1968 (1) M.L.J. 119. Under article 150, the power of proclamation of emergency is endowed with.

### 4.2.5 EMERGENCY POWERS

Article 150, which deals with emergency powers, reads as follows :-

"150. (1) If the Yang di-Pertaun Agong is satisfied that a grave emergency exists whereby the security or economic life of the Federation or any part thereof is threatened, he may issue a proclamation of emergency.

(2) If a proclamation of emergency is issued, when Parliament is not sitting, the Yang di-Pertaun Agong shall summon Parliament as may be practicable, and may until both the Houses of Parliament are sitting, promulgate ordinances having the force of law, if satisfied that immediate action is required.'

In this article there are 7 clauses and in reference to the judicial interpretations Lord President of the Federal Court, Malaysia, Tum Mohd.Suffian bin Hashim in his VV Chitaley Memorial Lectures, 1980, p.67, 68 and 69 (AIR publications) observed the following principles in this regards :-

(1) The King may proclaim an emergency only on advice, he can not act alone. This appears clear from 3 cases: Stephen Kalong Ningkan v. The Government of Malaysia, 1968, (1975).

(2) The courts will not review the validity of a proclamation of an emergency by enquiring whether in the circumstances, a state of emergency did exist - provided the proclamation appears *ex facie* to have been made in the manner required by the constitution. This decision follows two Privy Councils appeals from India, Bhagat Singh v The King Emperor (1931), 58 I.A. 169; The King Emperor Vs Benorari Lal Sharma (1945) A.C.14 (A.I.R. 1945 P.C.45).

(3) The courts' seem to favour a broad interpretation of the words, "Grave Emergency" of article 150. The Privy Council in The Stephen Kalong Ningkan Vs The Government of Malaysia (1968)p 241, 241, 2 M.L.J. said the term, "the emergency .....can not be confined to the unlawful use or threat of force in any of its manifestations .....although in emergency it is to be within that article must be not only grave but such as to threaten the security or economic life of the Federation or any part thereof. The natural meaning of the word itself is capable of covering a wide range of situations and occurrences, including such diversed events as wars, famines, earthquakes, floods, epidemics and the collapse of civil government. As Lord Ronadin observed when delivering the judgement of the board in Bhagat Singh and Ors Vs. The King emperor; `A state or emergency is something that does not permit of any exact definition: it connotes a state of matters calling for drastic action. ....".

(4) ............Power of the king to promulgate the orders.

(5) The Courts will not review the decision of the executive to issue emergency ordinances in the same way as they are unwilling to review the decisions on the issuing of proclamations of emergency.

(6) The courts have, however, once reviewed the validity of an emergency ordinance on the ground that the issuing authority has not complied with necessary formalities.'

He further states at p.72 ibid article 151 has come before the courts in several cases and the following summarises the attitudes of the courts: (1) The courts will not review the subjective satisfaction or the decision of the executive to detain a person.

"(2) ........... (6) ..............."

Therefore, in the above words of Lord President of the Federal Court Malaysia that there is no judicial review exercise on the proclamation of emergency under Malaysian constitution. But, however, it has not ruled out that the challenging of the validity of proclamation of emergency on the ground of mala fides. This has been made clear in the case of Stephen Klang Ningkan vs. Tun Abang Haji Obeng & Tawi Sli (No.2) (1967) p.337 to 338, the Constitution of Malaysia with development from 1957 to 1977, edited by Tun Mohamed Suffian, Lord President of the Federal Court of Malaysia, H.P.Lee, Lecturer in law, Monarch University, Melbourne and F.A.Trindade, Association Prof, Faculty of law, Monarch University, Melbourne published by Kuala Lumpur Oxford University Press, 1979, and this is referred to, in the words of Chief Justice Pike, that he felt the cases established that there could be no judicial review provided it (the proclamation), was made bona fide.

There is no exact provision of article 356 in the Malaysian constitution but however, on two occasions there were break down of governments in the States of Sarawak and Kelantan and whereby the article 150 was resorted to by the President of Malaysian Government i.e. Yang di-Pertuan Akong.

**4.2.6.1** In 1977, article 356 under which the power of the President to issue proclamation and thereby imposition of President's rule are challenged and came in for a far discussion in the Supreme Court of India in 1977.

The Supreme Court of India had taken up this issue for discussion comprising of M.H.Beg, C.J., Y.V.Chandrachud, P.N.Bhagawati, P.K.Goswami, A.C.Gupta, N.L.Untwala and S.Murtaza Fazal Ali, JJ. and the judgment was delivered on 6.5.1977 for original suits numbers 126 of 1977 and it is known as state of Rajasthan and Ors Vs. Union of India. Dr. Justice D.D.Basu, has briefly outlined the facts of the case in his comparative Constitutional Law in p.193 to 194 and it is as follows :-

"In short, *where that at the* 1977 election to the House of the People, the Janta party was returned by an overwhelming majority, completely routing the Congress R which however was in power in various states, including the northern states which brought the litigation in question. The Union Home Minister had issued a letter to the chief ministers of these states requesting them to advise their respective governors to dissolve the assemblies on the ground that the party in majority in those assemblies has lost confidence of the electorate, as evinced by the election to the House of the People. Some announcements by the Union Law Minister gave rise to apprehension that the President would be advised by the Union Cabinet to issue a proclamation under article 356 (1) and in pursuance thereof, directly dissolve the legislative assemblies, in case the chief ministers did not oblige by complying with the requests made in the letter addressed by the Union Home Minister. The court held that the letter which was in the nature of a request, did not offer any cause of action. Assuming that it was in the nature of directive and that, read with the attendant circumstances, it constituted a threat to apply article 356 (1) in order to dissolve the state legislative assemblies, the court held that the Constitution had conferred power upon the President to issue a proclamation under article 356 (1) upon his subjective satisfaction, which could not be questioned by the court, unless there was evidence of mala fides or a constitutional provision was violated by such action, which was absent in that current case. In coming to this conclusion, the majority of the judges observed that in order to form the subjective satisfaction, the President had to make an assessment of the political situation and take into consideration other factors which were not, in their nature, capable of being examined by the application of judicial methods, unless the circumstances as disclosed before the court clearly demonstrated that the President had acted on considerations extraneous to article 356 (1).

....... The legitimacy ......of the doctrine of political question in India, it would be useful to summarise some broad propositions which have, generally been established by consensus so far in the USA., and India:

(1) The legal interpretation of the constitution is in the exclusive domain of the court. (State of Rajasthan v Union of India, 1977 S.C.1361 and SP Gupta V UOI 1982 S.C.149).

(2) In India, this jurisdiction is vested the courts by various provisions of the constitution.

(3) From this function and duty to interpret the constitution evolves another function of the course, i.e., to demarcate the boundaries of the constitutional jurisdiction of the different organs of the state-executive, legislative and judicial in case of any conflict between them presented in justiciable form before a court.

(4) the court can not, accordingly, decline to examine whether any of the limitations imposed by the constitution has been violated by the executive "merely on the facile ground that the question is political in tone, colour or complexion" or on the ground that it would lead to a confrontation with another branch of the government.

(5) It is also true that in India, there is no rigid separation of powers between the three organs of the govt. as in the USA.

**4.2.6.2** In the case of state of Rajasthan v Union of India Chandrachud J., held that the grounds under which the executive power under article 356 to promulgate state of emergency on the breakdown of a constitutional machinery of a state are found genuine and there is no mala fide in the conclusion. In his words, 'the Home Minister's letter shows that (i) an unprecedented political situation had arisen by the virtual rejection, in the recent Lok Sabha elections, of candidates belonging to the ruling party in various states; (ii) the resulted climate of uncertainty was such as to cause grave concern; (iii) the situation had created a sense of diffidence at different levels of administration; (iv) people at large did not appreciate the propriety of continuance in power of a party which was unmistakably rejected by the electorate; and (v) the climate of uncertainty, diffidence and dis-respect had given rise to serious threat to law and order. It is on the basis of this reasons that the Home Minister concluded that a fresh appeal to the political sovereign was not only permissible but had become obligatory. These grounds, can not *with any show reason,* be dismissed as *baring* no rational nexus with a necessity for issuing a proclamation with a view to dissolving the legislative assemblies of the nine states. p. 125 of Supreme Court judgment of State of Rajasthan V UOI.

Therefore, to understand and identify whether there is any malȧ fide in the proclamation of ordinance and imposition of President's rule under article 356, the grounds under which executive power has been exercised or otherwise? In other words, it amounts to investigate and verify the subjective satisfaction of the President to conclude whether any event or events are otherwise that there has been a break down of constitutional machinery in a state and also the state machinery is unable to carry out the directives of the Union Government. If that is the interpretation, the decision of the Bhagat Singh Case has been overruled. And also it is equal to say that the political question is subject to judicial review. This paramount power given to the judiciary in the capacity of *"arbiter"* who interpret the provisions of the constitution. But, however, the interpretation of the constitutional provision does not conclude that it amounts to supervene other limbs of three divisions of power such as

(i) Legislative
(ii) Executive; and
(iii) Judiciary.

**4.2.6.3** This has been made clear in the judgment of case of United States v Butler (1935) 297, U.S.1, 87, as said by justice Harlan F.Stone in his oft-quoted descending opinion: "Courts are not the only agency of government that must be achieved to have the capacity to govern" ref. Para 126 ibid.

**4.2.6.4** In the same judgement J.Bhagwati for himself and on behalf of A.C.Gupta, J., held that there are two main questions which arrive for consideration in these suits and writ petitions, namely (i) Whether these suits are maintainable under article 131 and the writ petition under article 32; and

(ii) What is the scope and ambit of the power of the President under article 356 clause I and whether and if so, under what circumstances can the court interfere with the exercise of this power by the President.

With reference to the first question as it is not much relevant to our topic at this moment, we will concentrate on the second question. Bhagawati J., while examining the constitutional application of the executive power under article 356 clause I and in reference to article 174 class 2 (b) wherein which by virtue of exercising the power under article 356 clause I sub clause (a) the President can also dissolve the legislative assembly of the state by virtue of assuming all the powers of a governor including the power under article 174 clause 2 sub clause (b), the legislative assembly can be dissolved and all spheres of democratic experiment in federalism would be affected since this is very extra ordinary power which either could be used or abused. In this connection, Bhagawati J., quotes the words of Dr. Ambedkar, "I may say that I do not altogether deny that there is a possibility of these articles being abused or employed for political purposes. But the objection applies to every part of the constitution which gives power to the Centre to override the provinces. In fact, I share the sentiments expressed by my Hon'ble Friend Mr.Gupta yesterday that the property *we ought is expected* to that such articles will never be called into operations and that they would remain a dead letter. If at all they are brought into operation, I hope the President who is endowed. with these powers will take proper precautions before actually suspending the administration of the provinces.'

While falling in toe to the expressions of Dr.Ambedkar it will not be ridiculous to recollect the events of 1977 and events of 1980. In 1977, there was the dissolution of nine legislative assemblies by virtue of resorting to drastic power given to the President of India under article 356. The nine legislative assemblies which were dissolved were belonging to

Congress party. In 1980, the dissolved legislative assemblies by virtue of resorting to the extra ordinary power given under article 356 were belonging to other than Congress party which had won in the 1980 elections held in February, 1980. Therefore, it seems very clear that there could be no second opinion on the apprehension expressed by the founding fathers of the Indian Constitution. But it does not mean there is a mala fide in exercising the power under article 356.

"The proclamation issued by the President under article 356 clause 1 would cease to be in force at the expiration of two months unless it is approved by both the Houses of Parliament, and therefore, no irretrievable action such as dissolution of the legislative assemblies of the state can be taken by the President before the approval of the both Houses of Parliament is given to the proclamation. Otherwise the parliamentary control would be defeated and it would be possible for the Central Government to present *fait accompli* to the two House of Parliament and neither House would be able to remedy the mischief done, even if the proclamation is disapproved." Bhagwati J. held (para 138). Moreover, there is no single provision either under article 356 or elsewhere in the constitution that the power exercised under article 356 would be null and void as and when the Parliament disapproves or otherwise also there is no single provision in the Constitution that it is a must for exercising the power under article 356. Therefore, whatever is exercised is exercised under article 356. There the only problem is whether it should continue or otherwise? And that will be subject to the approval of the both the Houses of Parliament. This is also applicable for both, the article 356 and ordinance promulgating power of the President under article 356. It will be opt to quote the words of Bhagwati J., "To hold otherwise would be to refuse to give full effect to the proclamation which has pointed out above, continuous to operate with full force and eager during the period of two months. It would be re-writing article 356 and making approval of both the Houses of Parliament a condition precedent to the coming into force of the proclamation so far as the particular power is concerned. "p.140 ibid

**4.2.6.5** Bhagwati J. has also made it clear that how the court is unable to issue injunction so that the Union can be prevented from restraining the power under article 356 to dissolve the legislative assembly. To quote, "Turning to the relief sought against the threatened exercise of power under article 356 clause 1 we find that what is prayed for in this relief is "permanent injunction restraining the defendants from taking the recourse under article 356 of the Constitution of India to dissolve the legislative assembly of the states and from taking any steps from holding fresh election to the state assembly March of 1977". It is indeed difficult to appreciate how such a wide and sweeping injunction can be granted by this court restraining the Union of India exercising altogether its powers under article 356 clause 1." Probably, this particular point of contention is emanating in view of article 365 where it is the constitutional duty of the Union of India to protect and ensure that the government of states carry out in accordance with the provisions of the constitution and duty of the Union to protect the state against an external aggression and internal disturbance under article 355. Bhagwati J. states "How can the Union of India be prevented by this court from discharging its constitutional obligation to the states. We have already pointed out that there is a constitutional duty enjoined on the Union of India to ensure that the government of every state is carried on in accordance with the provisions of the constitution and there is equally a constitutional obligation on the President, that is the Central Government to take action under article 356 clause 1 if he finds that a situation has arisen when the government of the state can not be carried on in accordance with the provisions of the constitution.' p.142 ibid.

While deliberating on this point Bhagwati J. holds a very strong view on the decision of King Emperor vs. Banoarilal Sharma, 72 Ind. App. 57 (AIR 1945 p 48) where "Viscount Simon, L.C. agreed that the Governor-General declaring that *emergency exists* must act bonafide and in accordance with his statutory powers. This is the narrow minimal area in which the exercise of power under article 356 clause 1 is subject to judicial review. And apart from it, it can not rest with the court to challenge the satisfaction of the President that the situation contemplated in the clause exists." p.144 ibid. The grounds which are becoming compulsions on the part of the President of India to conclude where there a grave situation exists and that amounts to failure of constitutional machinery can be attributed to be of political questions which can not be questioned. In this reference, Bhagwati J. states, "......These are all consequences which can not be said to be unlikely to arise from such an unusual state of affairs and they make it impossible for the govt. of state to be carried on in accordance with the provisions of the constitution. Whether the situation is fraught with such consequences are not entirely a matter of political judgment for the executive branch of the government." And finally he quotes, "we hold that on the facts and circumstances of the present case this ground is clearly a relevant ground having regard to which the President is required to be satisfied before taking action under article 356 clause 1" p.147 ibid.

**4.2.6.6** Goswami J. also agrees to same conclusions stating, "I am not prepared to say that this court, which is the last recourse for the oppressed and the bewildered, will, for good, refuse to consider when there may be sufficient materials to establish that proclamation under article 356 clause 1 is tented with the mala fides. I would, however, hasten to add that the grounds given in the Home Minister's letter can not by any stretch of imagination be held to be mala fide or extraneous or irrelevant. These grounds will have reasonable nexus with the subject of a proclamation under article 356 of clause 1 of constitution." p.117 ibid.

**4.2.6.7** Untwala J. while analysing the challenges filed in suits and writs on the doors which were closed for the courts to enter the prohibited area and is popularly called the political field, refers to the certain constitutional decisions. He proceeds that "......the necessity of entering the prohibited field to peep into the reality of the situation by examination of the facts by themselves, either on the ground of legality or mala fides the courts havė always resisted and shall continue to resist the inducement to enter the prohibit field: for example, Lakhi Narayan Das v The Province of Bihar 1949 F.C.R. 693 (AIR 1950 F.C.59) and M/s.S.K.G.Sugar Ltd., v state of Bihar 1975 1 S. C.R.312 (AIR 1974 sc 1533). To put it graphically clause 5 has merely put a seal on such close to doors to check more emphatically the temptation or the urge to make the court enter the prohibited field. Attempts have always been made by the party who is out of the field of power, if I can equate it with the prohibit field aforesaid, to induce the court to enter that field in order to relief against the taking of the extra ordinary steps by the President on the advise of the governor in power. On the other hand, party in power has always resisted such move. In a democracy, the current of public opinion and franchise may push a particular ship on the side of the shore or the other. But this court, like the Pole star, has to guide and has guided the path of all marines in an even remaining aloof from the current and irrespective of the fact whether a particular ship is on this shore or that. "p.178 ibid.

**4.2.6.8** In continuation of his argument on exercise of judicial review he states, "In reference to the issue of justiciability the words of Lord Mac Dermott in the case of Stephen Kelong Ningkan v Government of Malaysia 1970 AC 379 at p.391-92: " The issue of justiciability raised by the Govt of Malaysia led to difference of opinion in Federal Court, the Lord President of Malaysia and the Chief Justice of Malaya holding that the validity of the proclamation was not justiciable and Ong J. holding that it was. Whether a proclamation under statutory powers by the Supreme Head of the Federation can be challenged before the court on some or any grounds is a constitutional question of far reaching importance which, on the present state of the authorities remains unsettled and debatable."

".... I could rest content by saying that, as a view facts placed before us are exclusively within the prohibited area". p.179 ibid.

**4.2.6.8** Fazal Ali J., referred to the judgment of a Division Bench of the Kerala High Court in K.K.Aboo V UOI, AIR 1965 Kerala 229 at p.239 and in which the court observed as follows :

"Article 356 1 (b) empowers the President whenever he satisfied of a constitutional break down in the state, to issue a proclamation declaring inter alia, "that the powers of the legislature of the state shall be exercisable by or under the authority of Parliament". That necessarily implies a power to dissolve the state legislature. No resort therefore need be had by the President to the provisions of article 356 1 (a) read with article 172 or article 174 to dissolve the states legislative assembly. The power to dissolve the state legislature is implicit in article 356 1(b) itself." And while concurring the above verdict, Fazal Ali J., states that 'I fully endorsed the aforesaid observations which laid down the correct law on the subject on this particular aspect of the matter.' p.210 ibid.

Further, Fazal Ali J., states ".......I am clearly of the opinion that the article 356 1 (a) confers the powers of the governor under article 174 (2) or the President in clear and categorical terms and I can not infer exclusion of the power merely from the fact that the proclamation is to expire after two months. Even if the order dissolving the assembly can not be ratified by the Parliament under clause 3 does not touch actions taken, proceedings completed, consequences ensured and orders ensured. At the time when Parliament exercises the control, all these actions have already taken place and it is not possible to put the clock back or to reverse actions which have already been taken and completed, nor was such a contingency contemplated by the founding fathers of the constitution." p.211 ibid.

With the above mentioned reasons in support of the unanimous order passed by this court on April 29, 1977 dismissing the suits and writ petitions and rejecting the prayers or injunction and interim reliefs.

**4.2.6.9** In the High Court of Karnataka, there was a case on the same in reference to the proclamation of emergency power under article 356 to impose President's rule in state of Karnataka and for which the judgement was delivered on 4.8.1989 which was published in AIR 1990 Karnataka 5. The name of the case is S.R.Bommai and Ors. V UOI and Ors. The case was taken up by full bench of the Karnataka High Court comprising of Prem Chand Jain Chief Justice, N.Venkatachala and K.Shivashankar Bhat JJ. The proclamation of imposition of President's rule in state of Karnataka was challenged on the grounds of legal mala fides. The court held:-

(1) That the proclamation made under article 356 of the constitution is justiciable and that the courts could look into the materials or the reasons disclosed for issuing the proclamation, to find out whether those materials or reasons were wholly extraneous to the formation of the satisfaction and had no rational nexus at all to the satisfaction reached under article 356 of the constitution.

(2) That under article 356 (1) the President has to be satisfied on the basis of the report received from the governor or otherwise that the govt. of state can not be carried on in accordance with the provisions of the constitution. The satisfaction of the President should be the result of comprehending in his own way the facts and circumstances relevant to the subjective satisfaction. The satisfaction is to be of the President and the President alone. President means the Council of Ministers.

(8) That in law the legal mala fides which vitiate the impugned proclamation should be attributable to the President or the Union Council of Ministers who in reality exercise the power under article 356. Hence in our view sending of a report by the governor to the President invoking exercise of his power under article 356 (1) can not be a ground for holding that the impugned proclamation is one which is tented with the legal mala fides.

(9) That the view we have taken on the material disclosed that the same is relevant that the subjective satisfaction arrived at by the President is conclusive and there is no scope at all

for a finding the action of the President is in flagrant violation of the very words of article 356 (1), ......

(10) That the basic fact to be determined is the relevance of the grounds disclosed and if the same are to be found relevant then no exceptions can be taken to the exercise of power under article 356 (1)." p.38 of the judgement of SR Bommai V UOI AIR 1990 Karnataka 5.

The court itself has stated "As our order is solely based on the decision of the Supreme Court in Rajasthan case AIR 1977 SC 1361.".

# 5

# The MP High Court Judgment in Patwa Vs. Union of India, March 1993 A Criticism

**5.1.1** On April 2, 1993, the MP High Court consisting of Chief Justice S.K.Jha, B.M.Dharmadhikari J. and K.M.Agrawal J. by majority of two to one held that proclamation issued by the President of India on December 15, 1992 imposing President's rule in exercise of power under article 356 in Madhya Pradesh and dissolves state assembly should quashed and issued directions for reinstatement of government and revival of state 'vidhan sabha'. (April 3, 1993, The Hitavada, Nagpur). The majority judgement went into 35 pages and dissending judgment by justice Agrawal ran into 18 pages.

**5.1.2** Therefore, 4 sets of petition out of which the main was filed by Mr. Sundar Lal Patwa, outgoing chief minister of Madhya Pradesh who had alleged in the petition that there was no material available with the central govt. to show that the govt. could not be run in accordance with the provisions of the constitution. The three reports and other informations furnished by the governor was only to the effect that there were riots at Bhopal and Ujjain but the outbreak of the riots, which were subsided in a course of few days, alone can not be equated to the failure of the constitutional machinery. Solicitor General of India Shri D.Gupta, who had specially come from Delhi to Jabalpur to argue this on behalf of the Central Govt urged the following three points in the main:

(1) That the matter is not justiciable.,

(2) That the matter which was available with the govt. is a privileged one and can not be asked to be discussed and,

(3) That the totality of the circumstances resulting in riots in Bhopal and Ujjain were sufficient to arrive at a conclusion that there has been a failure of the constitutional machinery in the state of Madhya Pradesh.

**5.1.3** The Hon'ble judges held in a majority view that the matter is justiciable and the materials available on record proved that discrimination was made between the outbreak of riots at one or two places in Madhya Pradesh where 100 of other cities in the same states were free from communal troubles. In their concluding para of 35 page judgment, it was held that their Lordship quashed and impugned the proclamation of the President's rule in state of Madhya Pradesh under article 356. (April 3, 1993, The Hitavada, Nagpur).

The court kept the operation of its verdict in abeyance for two weeks to allow the Union Government to prefer an appeal to Supreme Court. Mr. Tulsi, Addl. solicitor General of India who was present in the court made an oral prayer for his certificate of fitness for appeal in the Supreme Court and he also prayed for one week's interim stay of the order. In response the court granted the fitness certificate for appeal and stayed the operation of order for two weeks.

**5.1.4** According to MP High Court judgment the case of Sundar Lal Patwa v•UOI decided on 2nd April, 1993, there are two legal aspects such as follows :-

(1) In the information available or the grounds which were taken for consideration by the President of India while exercising the emergency power under article 356 were not found sufficient to bring a rational nexus between the grounds for subjective satisfaction and the necessity of resorting to the dangerous power rested with the Union under article 356 amounting to dissolution of legislative assembly of Madhya Pradesh and imposition of President's rule. In this context, the court has been of the view that the alternative measures like despatching more CRPF Jawans or BSF or other para military forces to contain the communal riots would have been most appropriate than resorting to use of article 356. This is in consonance with article 355 where it is the duty of the union to protect the state government from external aggression and internal disturbance.

(2) Since the proclamation of President's rule in the state of Madhya Pradesh under article 356 is void *ab initio*, the dissolved state legislative assembly of Madhya Pradesh should be restored.

### 5.2.1 CRITICISMS

**5.2.2** According to the case of state of Rajasthan v UOI AIR 1977 1361 as Fazal Ali J. puts that "I am clearly of the opinion that the article 356 1 (a) confers the powers of the governor under article 174 (2) or the President in clear and categorical terms and I can not infer exclusion of the power merely from the fact that the proclamation is to expire of two months. Even if the order dissolving the assembly can not be ratified by the Parliament under clause 3 of article 356 that makes no difference, because clause 3 does not touch actions taken, proceedings completed, consequences ensured and orders ensured. At the time when Parliament exercises the control all these actions have already taken place and it is not possible to put the clock back or to reverse actions which have already been taken and completed, nor was such a contingency contemplated by the founding fathers of the constitution." p.211 ibid. Therefore, the Supreme Court, the highest judicial authority of India has been of the clear vision that it is not possible to put the clock back or to reverse actions which have been taken and completed and if that is so it is not convincing to understand and appreciate even taken for granted the nullity of the presidential proclamation order of imposition of President's rule under article 356 could be made acceptable but it could not be the fact that the dissolved state legislative assembly could be revived on any account. Further, Fazal Ali, J. stresses that the founding fathers have well thought of it, it is not something unusual of it.

**5.2.3** In the Constitution Assembly Debate on the report of the Union Constitution Committee under Part VIII (A) emergency powers Shri K.Santhanam in the following words :-

"(1) If at any time, the governor of a province is satisfied that a situation has arisen in which the government of the province can not be carried on in accordance with the provisions of this constitution and has so reported to the President of the Federation or is the President of the Federation is satisfied that the normal government of the province has broken down, he may take any action which he considers necessary including

(1) suspension of the provincial constitution

(2) promulgation of the ordinance to be applicable to the province: and

(3) issuing of orders and instructions to the governor and other officials of the province.

When any such action is taken by the President, he shall report to the federal legislature and unless his action is ratified by both the Houses of legislature within a period of six months from the date of his taking action the normal constitution of the province shall be restored. The situation shall be reviewed by the Federal legislature and continuation, if necessary, of the emergency action approved every six months

**5.2.4** The President shall restore the normal constitution as soon as he is satisfied that the emergency has ceased to exist. p. 1948-1949 Vol.I from 912.1946 to 23.12.1946 Constituent

Assembly Debate Official Report reprinted by Lok Sabha Secretariat New Delhi 1985.

**5.2.5** Shri B.M.Gupta moved another new part of the provision of the emergency power and as it runs, "(1) (i) on report being made by a governor of a province under section.... of this constitution the President of the Federation shall have the power to issue, in consultation with his council of ministers, a proclamation assuming to himself or any of the powers vested in or exercisable by any provincial body or authority except the High Court, including the power to control, modify or revoke the proclamation issued by the governor.

(ii) The proclamation under this section shall cease to operate at the expiration of two months unless it continuous for any further period is approved from time to time by a resolution passed by the Federal Legislature "p. 949 ibid.

**5.2.6** The power of governor to issue proclamation of emergency power is in reference to the memorandum on the principles of a model provincial constitution under the Chairmanship of Hon'ble Sardar Vallabhbhai Patel for Provincial Constitutional Committee appendix No.CA 64/Cons/47 Constitution Assembly of India 27th June, 1947, New Delhi that there will be a governor of a province who will be endowed with a special responsibility namely the prevention of any grave menace to the peace and tranquility of the province or any part thereof and in the discharge of his discretion. Therefore, the power exercised by the governor could be reviewed or modified by the President of the Federation. somehow, after long deliberations the idea of entrusting the emergency power to the governor has been dropped and entrusted with only the President of the Federation. This is being reflected also in the draft article 278 of the Constitution of India which has become article 356 of the present Constitution of India. Here the point of consideration is right from the earlier discussion to the draft article discussion there had been disputes on three counts;

(1) whether the emergency power should be given to the governors or otherwise both the President and governor;
(2) whether the President alone should be given the emergency powers; and
(3) the period for the endorsement of the federal legislature whether to be six months or two months.

Finally, including in the draft article 278 and in the present article 356 all these points are made clear by stating that the endorsement of the Parliament is compulsory for the continuance beyond two months, and only the President is given the power to exercise the emergency power under article 356. The President alone can not function but only under aid and advice of the Council of Ministers. Therefore, nowhere it is mentioned that Parliament can nullify the powers already exercised by the President of India under article 356 right from the date of promulgation of the imposition of President's rule in a state till two months for which for every continuance a separate resolution has to be passed by both the Houses of Parliament and if the Houses of Parliament do not pass such a resolution for its continuance, the proclamation of the imposition of President's rule under article 356 is expired after two months. Therefore, Bhagwati J has aptly said in the case of state of Rajasthan V UOI "The proclamation issued by the President under article 356 clause it would cease to be in force at the expiration of two months unless it is approved by both the Houses of Parliament, and therefore, no irretrievable action such as dissolution of the legislative assemblies of the state can be taken by the President before the approval of the both House of Parliament is given to the proclamation. "para 138, that anything other than this would amount to re-writing article 356 and the constitution.

**5.2.7** The MP High Court has not only entered into the prohibited area with less caution and concern but also has suggested other alternative measures which would have been more suitable rather than resorted to article 356. Untwalia J. in the Rajasthan case refers to the Prohibited Field - Seervai Volume II P. 2205-06 however takes the position that the political doctrine which is passed on and is a consequence of rigid separation of powers - a future noticable in the US Constitution - has no place in our constitution which is not based on rigid separation of powers doctrine. A well known view of the doctrine puts it tensily thus; "the political question/ doctrine is thus a way of avoiding a principled decision damaging to the court or an expeditent decision damaging to the principle" (Constitution of U.S.A. - Analysis and Interpretation - quoted in Seervai at Page 2208) - The classicalist or classicist position, however, is that courts are duty bound to decide all cases properly before them. (But what is a case in the sense of being a justiciable controversy when is a case "properly" before the court? These terms beg the question". In Bakker vs Carr, Brennan J., speaking for majority in the U.S. Supreme Court stated that the several formulations as to what is a political question have all elements which identify it as essentially a function of the separation of powers. Prominent on the face of such question one can discover in the famous words of Brennan J. a "textually demonstrable constitutional commitment of the issue to a coordinate political department", or a lack of judicially discoverable or manageable standard of decision; or the impossibility of deciding without an intial policy determination of a kind clearly for not justiciable discretion a political question is one which a judge choses not to decide of political nature or the impossibility of a court undertaking an independent resolution without expressing lack of respect due to coordinate branch of government; or an unusal need for unquestioning adherence to a political decision already made; or the potentiality of pronouncements by various departments on political question." In Bakker Vs Carr, Frank Furter J. dissented stating that apportionment of electoral districts is a political question to be settled without judicial interference. This is almost the political function of the government by the judiciary which will not be in good spirit if the viewpoints expressed here would be taken into account as stated in supremacy of Law in Malaysia by Duli Yang Maha Mulia, Journal of Malaysian Constitutional Law, 1984 at page

6, "By way of digression, let me relate to you a little bit of English constitutional history. In the old days Kings of England exercised Supreme Executive Power in the Land. The Courts were historical the King's court and the judges were always the King's judges. The King appointed the judges and the King at one time could remove them at his pleasure. On one occasion King James 1 summoned all the judges before him and told them that he proposed to take any case as he may please the way from the judges for decision and to try them himself. But Chief Justice Sir Edward Coke told the King that he had no power to do so, and that all cases ought to be determined in a court of justice and according to the law and custom of the realm. King James replied, "I always thought I have often heard the boost that your English Law is founded upon reason. If that be so, why have not I and others reasoned as well as you the judges?"

**5.2.8** The Chief Justice replied, "True, it is, please your Majesty that God had endowed your Majesty with excellent signs as well as great gifts of nature; but your Majesty will allow me to say so, with all reverence, that you are not learned in the law of this your realm of England...... which is an art which requires long study and experience before that a man can attend to the cognizance of it. The law is the golden melwand and measure to try the causes of your Majesty's subject, and it is by that law that your Majesty is protected in safety and peace.'

**5.2.9** King James, in a great rage, said, "Then I am to be under the law- which it is treason to affirm."

**5.3.1** Chief Justice replied in the words of Bracton that the King is under no man, but under God and the law."

**5.3.2** This conveys only one thing that the executive can not execute the role of judiciary interpreting law and to act as custodian of the constitution and interpreter of the constitution. But at the same time, the judges or the judiciary can not supervene the realm of executive. It is well quoted in

Shri Lembah case by the judge who is the author of this article at Page No. 149: "Government of judges would be regarded as an usurpation of legislative authority."

**5.3.3** This is in the State of Rajasthan V UoI. Untwala J. in para 178, "To put it graphically clause 5 has merely put a seal on such closed doors to check more emphatically the temptation on the urge to make the courts enter the prohibited field. Attempts have always been made by the party who is out of the field of power, if I can equate it with the prohibited field aforesaid, to induce the court into enter that field in order to give relief against the taking of the extra ordinary steps by the President on the advice of the government in power."

**5.3.4** But at the same it is also the fact that "One of the most difficult problems of judicial review, and also one of the most intriguing, is the perennial uncertainty over its boundaries", as quoted by Robert Ward, in his article on Judicial Review and Trials on Indictment: Section 29(3) of the Supreme Court Act, 1981, published by in Pubic Law, 1988. Thus, eventhough it is a prohibited area despite of every caution and concern the inherent limitation certainly has to be overcome, but not nevertheless overruled.

**5.3.5** Because of this limitation it would be unfortunate that the judicial review should be forthwith taken away from the competence of judiciary. And also it would be improper to leave it to the decisive overtone of executive predominance. In this respect, it will be opt to quote the words of Monahan and Peter in his article of Developments in Constitutional Law, 85-86 term, 9, S.C.L.Rev (69), 1987, as referred ny Jamie Cassels in "Judicial activism and Public interest Litigation in India: Attempting the impossible?", pp 495-96, The American Journal of Comparative Law, Vol 37, 1989, "A purely negative understanding of liberty, wherein governmental action is portrayed as the primary enemy of human freedom, leads to the view that the only function of judicial review is to police those very forms of collective action which are necessary to retrace inequality". And it will be more appropriate where we are subject to parliamentary democracy and thereby the views of the majority electors form the nature and constituent elements of ruling party in the government and also the executives both as Head of State and Head of Government. Eventhough it may not be true in terms of its value but nevertheless it can not be ciphered off. To quote in the words of P.P.Criec, "Democracy did not embody compromise, but imply a monopoly of power by one half of the people over the other half", in Unitary, Self-Collecting Democracy in the Law quarterly review, Jan, 1990, p.136. The same view is further supported in the words of W.S.Mckechnie, in "The democracy under constitution 1912, p.164, "There is no justification, either in reason, equity, custom or common sense for a political system which places the liberty and property lives and honour of one half of the community absolutely and legally at the mercy of the other half." This is most relevant to quote where there is the discretionary power embodied in the provisions of the Indian Constitution to the executives. It so happen in 1979, the President Sanjiv Reddy, who adopted to his discretionary power and invited Mr. Charan Singh, a break-way group of Janta party to form the Cabinet and Head the Government despite of the fact that Shri Jagjivan Ram who has been holding majority of the Janta party MPs of about 200 with able support from other like minded parties. Again it so happened in the year 1990, Shri R.Venkataraman, the President of India invited Shri Chandra Shekhar who has got the support of only 56 MPs to form the Government at the Centre by applying to the discretionary power incorporated in the Constitution of India article 75 to appoint the Prime Minister that "the Prime Minister shall be appointed by the President". Similar to it, it also happened in 1951, the governor of Madras invited Mr. Rajagopalachari of Congress party the leader of the largest single party to form the government and rejected the claim of Mr. T.Prakasam who had formed a new party having the support of 167 members in the House of 375 members. The Congress had the strength of only 155. (Ref.p. 281-287, Constitutional Law of India, Dr. J.N.Pandey, 1991 edition, Central Law Agency, Allahabad).

**5.3.6** Therefore, necessarily there has to be a kind of check which could safeguard and protect the Constitution of India and that is the role given to the judiciary in India. But, however, who had exceeded the prohibited area both in respect of legislature or executive or by the judiciary itself could not be easily identified. In this respect, it will be more interesting to quote the words of Glan Ville Williams, Vol.52, Modern Law Review March 1981 p.179, "Which of you did it?

Sometimes one person of a pair or one of a group, must have offended but it is impossible to establish which it was. Each of the suspects may put the blame on another. Or each may try to protect both himself and others by remaining mum. This course is likely to frustrate the prosecution. The police may have a strong suspicion of the bunch in particular, but failing a reasonable prospect of getting a conviction there is doubtedly any point in bringing proceedings.

**5.3.7** Of course, charges based on strong suspicion sometimes succeeds. A former cause celebre on the subject, known to generations of students of Kenny's case was Manning (1849, The Times October 21, 1849, London), the facts contained all the ingredients of malo drama. A Custom officer was murdered in the Manning's house, where he had been invited to dinner. He was Mrs Manning's paramour. His dead body buried under the kitchen floor, and husband and wife then fled from London. The murder must have been committed by one or the other or both and both were charged. Council for the Mann suggested that the woman alone committed the murder, her object being robbery. Council for the woman suggested that the crime had been committed by the man alone, in a paroxysm of jealousy. Pollock L.C.B. directed that jury to consider whether, seeing that the murder was committed in the House where both the prisoners lived, it could possible have been undertaken by one without the knowledge of the other. Both the defendants were convicted and hanged."

**5.3.8** By virtue of the above analysis, it will not be good enough to leave it untouched as a No-Man Land. This has never been accepted in the course of history of any country in the world. Justice J.C.Shah, (Retd) in his lecture series subsequently published as the Rule of Law and the Indian constitution 1972 by N.M. Tripathi Pvt. Ltd., Bombay has said relevantly that, "That the power of judicial review varies from country to country. .......

But even in the United States the power of judicial review was evolved gradually and in the teeth of severe opposition. It took more than three quarters of a century for the Supreme Court of the United States to make an effective order invalidating a federal legislative measure. It was Chief Justice Marshall who firmly enunciated the doctrine of judicial review in Marbury v Madison, 1 Cranch 137. ........... "pp.84-85.

**5.3.9** Shah J., further narrates what kind of opposition has to be faced with that "A motion to impeach Chief Justice" was there but however, it, "proved aport. Impeachment proceedings where in fact commenced against judge Samuel Chase but they entered in acquittal and the ambition of President Jafferson to unseat Marshall had to be abandoned". p.87. Chief Justice Marshall could enunciate this doctrine of judicial review with extreme caution and concern since it is a prohibited area.

This particular spiels of causion and concern has been found forgotten in the judgments of MP High Court in the case of Patwa Vs. UoI.

# 6

# Perspectives on the Future Use of Article 356 A Suggested Framework

**6.1.1** In India, the constitution is the supreme. In other words, constitution is the embodiment of the supremacy of the law. The concept of the supremacy of the law has been an idea which we owe to the middle edges. In this regard it will be most reminding us the evolution of the supremacy of the law as an idea which had been the main theme portrayed in History of English Law in Vol.1 P. 182 of Pollack and Maitland and it has been referred in the Paper "The Law and the Constitution which was read by the Hon'ble Owen Dixon published in October, 1935, the Law quarterly review, p.591. This reads as. "There were times when Western Christendom was regarded as a single society with the temporal head whose imperium involved no effective power; the immediate allegiance of the individual was to a Lord who in turn was responsible to him for security and justice; local and special jurisdictions where they ruled. In such conditions, it was natural to conceive the law as the supreme authority governing the relations of all those who possessed power, whether king, prince or Lord as well as the position of those in complete subjection. Then no one could question the principle that the law was above the King. The conception had not appeared of the sovereign state in which there must be some repository of uncontrolled power."

Further it is also found in the classic text of Bracton who was the great institutional writer of the 13th Century and who was one of the Henry III's justices, that the King is below the law.

**6.1.2** In the British Constitutional Theory, the legal doctrine embodied in the revolution settlement by which three rival conceptions were reconciled and these three conceptions are

(1) The Supremacy of the Law;
(2) The Supremacy of the Crown; and
(3) The Supremacy of the Parliament.
(ref. p. 191 ibid)

**6.1.3** Keeping in continuity of this proposition the 20th Century legal scientist Prof.Ronald Dworkin in his Law's Empire 1986 said that we are all subject to the emperor rule of law - we live in the House of Law. And further he states that this means that a prescription is imposed upon us (from where presumably only God knows) which binds us to dwell not in the House of Lord, but under the aegis of the next best thing the House of Laws. (ref. Dwelling on the Threshold, Critical Essays on Modern Legal Thought by Allen C.Hutchinson, Carswell Co., Ltd., and Sweet and Maxual Ltd., Toronda & London, 1988).

In the same Book, author states, "If God destroyed the Tower of Babel because human doings were getting to close his own dwelling, then this collection of devils seem bent upon on destroying the palace built in God's own image. It is not quite clear what the mal-contents want. Some want only to repair the temple; others want to destroy what it exists and simply dancing the ruins; still others wish to tear to the ground the existing temple and build a new one."

**6.1.4** Definitely, our earnest attempt is not to destroy the temple; not even to do dance in the ruins but our endeavour is to preserve the existing temple and if it is in need in addition to the temple of Babel another temple can be constructed along with. Therefore, our efforts are to suggest the measures that could be more appropriately applied within the existing frameword of the constitution and also as an alternative model to the existing framework of the constitution which may require amendment to the constitution or that could be incorporated with the judicial law making efforts of the judiciary itself.

## 6.2 *SUGGESTIONS WITH IN THE EXISTING CONSTITUTIONAL FRAMEWORK*

**6.2.1 (A)** In Indian constitutional history, there had been limitless carry forward and backward entries in the annals of judicial pronouncements with reference to the power of the Parliament to amend the constitution. This problem could be amicably settled and the findings of the Supreme Court could become more acceptable to legal experts, constitutional scientists, parliamentarians and judges. This is the case of Keshvanand Bharati wherein a novel theme of basic structure was propounded within the existing framework of the constitution. Similarly, Chief Justice Marshall had propounded judicial review within the existing framework of the constitution. similarly, Chief Justice Marshall could propound the Doctrine of Judicial Review in a more subtle but with all force in the case of Marbury V Madisan. Therefore, what is required is not to overrun behind the prohibited area or to build a castle beyond the boundaries of judicial review. To go by within the framework of the constitution as per the judicial interpretation found in the Supreme Court majority judgement of state of Rajasthan vs. UoI that there is judicial review on the power exercised by the Executive under article 356 and it is justiciable in the court of law. Further to add, the court is having every right to strike down the proclamation order under article 356 when there are mala fides. With reference to subjective satisfaction of the President on the failure of the

Constitutional machinery of a State the grounds attributed must possess rational nexus. But definitely there should not be an effort in the name of judicial review to suggest alternative measures or put the clock back as well said in the case of state of Rajasthan v UoI. This would have been avoided better in the case of Sunder Lal Patwa v UoI by MP High Court in its judicial pronouncement. Since there has been not much visible concern and caution while dwelling upon the prohibited area. It would not be proper but however, it may not be improper to state that misguided power is more dangerous than unguided power. If such a situation repeats, that would be nothing but destroying the palace.

In addition to above, these are the following additional suggestions :-

**6.2.2 (1)** While exercising judicial review on the political questions the High Court can always refer such cases to the Supreme Court for further scrutinisation and application of interpretation where there is violation in the power given under article 356. By resorting to this, the Supreme Court of India may convene a fuller bench of the maximum of 17 or otherwise to deliberate on this so that a viable judicial interpretation could be evolved as in the case of basic structure theory in Keshvanand Bharati's case. In this point of reference the author may be permitted to quote the words of Woodrow Wilson observed in 1908 that "Whether by force or circumstance or by deliberated design, we have married legislation with adjudication and look for statesmanship in our courts". p.168 Constitutional government in the United States and at page 158 it is also found that the constitution "is not a mere lawyers document but is the vehicle of a nation's life." ibid. The very object is that the judiciary should evolve unhesitantly such a judicial interpretation which will invoke faith and confidence both in the executives, legislators, electors and judges themselves that the judicial finding is more appropriate to the needs of today and tomorrow. But at the same time, it may be reminded that the efforts put in for Nobeldream should not result in Nightmare as cautioned by

Prof.Hart on the activism of Supreme Court of USA. This is more appropriately applicable to the Supreme Court of India and down below it.

**6.2.3 (2)** Where there is mala fide in exercise of this power of article 356, the High Court can strike down the presidential proclamation order issued under article 356; give directives for election within the stipulated period of two months in the respective states and put an embargo on the Parliament not to endorse such promulgation order stating the proclamation is void *ab initio.*

**6.2.4 (3)** As the case of discussions in the Constituent Assembly Debates the governor or the President of India may issue memos to the respective states for suitable corrective measures or the governor or the President of India may give directives to carry out corrective measures within the stipulated time schedule framework so that the state government is given an opportunity to realise where the things have gone wrong.

**6.2.5 (4)** Apart from above mentioned, instead of dissolving assembly, the governor may be instructed to dismiss the existing cabinet with the chief minister and offer an opportunity to the ruling party which is enjoying majority in the state assembly to form a different ministry excluding those members of the council of ministers or otherwise opportunity may be given to other single largest part to explore possibility of forming alternative government. When these both efforts are failed then probably the dissolution of legislative assembly may be resorted to.

## 6.3 (B) SUGGESTIONS OVER AND ABOVE THE EXISTING FRAMEWORK OF THE CONSTITUTION

**6.3.1 (1)** Following the model of constitutional court of Germany or following the model of the latest constitutional court of the Republic of Korea which came into existence by an amendment to the constitution of April 1988 by incorporating three articles namely

(i) Article 111 of the constitution envisaged the jurisdiction of the court under five categories given below :-

(1) Questions of constitutionality of laws upon request of the courts
(2) Impeachment
(3) Dissolution of political parties
(4) Competence disputes between state organ; and
(5) Constitutional petitions.

The composition of the Constitution court is as follows :-

Three judges are nominated by the President, three by the Chief Justice of the Supreme Court and three by the National Assembly. The Presiding Justice of the court is designated by the President with the consent of the National Assembly.

Article 112 fixed the tenure of the Justices at six years with re-appointment.

The third and final article is article 113 that quorum of the decision is stated. According to article 113, atleast six of the nine justices must concur on constitution court decisions accepting cases presenting inter governmental jurisdiction disputes, in which case a simple majority is sufficient. These above mentioned articles came into force in August 5, 1988, It is true that the Supreme Court does have the same jurisdiction of the Constitutional Court of the Republic of Korea and thus, the conflict between the New Constitutional Court and the Supreme Court remain unresolved.

Taking into account of these above models, it is suggested that the constitution can be amended with the following provisions :-

(1) There should be constitutional council within the Supreme Court of India. This is proposed in order to remove such conflict found in the Constitutional Court of Republic of Korea.

(2) This Constitutional Council will be presided over by the elected Member of the Parliament in case the Chief Justice not presiding over the Constitutional Council.

(3) The composition of Constitutional Council is as follows :

(i) Six senior most justices of the Supreme Court of India nominated by the Chief Justice;

(ii) Four Chief Justices of high courts nominated by the Chief Justice of India in consultation with the President of India.

(iii) Three Members of Parliament nominated by the speaker of the Lok Sabha and of which in the order of largest single party each party will be represented.

(iv) Three members of Parliament nominated by the Chairman of the Rajya Sabha giving preference to the legal experts, law professors, social scientist or any other experts but however, it should be related to the largest political parties in order of their size, representation should be given.

(4) The quorum of the decision should be 2/3 majority.

(5) The subject matters meant for the jurisdiction of the Constitutional Council are as follows :-

(i) emergency powers under articles 352, 356, 360, etc.

(ii) Appointment of the Prime Minister or chief minister where the executive i.e., the President or the governor whoever exercises his discretionary power in appointing when there is no clear majority.

(iii) The issues pertaining to defection of legislators and members of Parliament.

(iv) The disputes on election commission functioning.

(6) Term of office should be in the order of their respective elections and appointment, e.g., the judges as per their normal term of office in the courts, the members of Parliament in Rajya Sabha and Lok Sabha respectively on their terms of office and also the Chief Justices of high courts.

(7) The decision of the Constitutional Council is binding on all the parties to the disputes.

(8) Pay and perks - As applicable to respective appointments and elections but in addition to above the separate annual payments my be made including for pensionary benefits.

(9) After serving for a term or a period there is no renomination or re-appointment to the Constitutional Council.

(10) The Constitutional Council will enjoy all the powers which are accorded any Supreme Court or high court decisions for its enforceability.

**6.3.2 II.** In addition to the above suggested within the existing constitutional framework an amendment can be made so as to provide as far as the endorsement of the proclamation of presidential rule under article 356 even for article 352 it is compulsory for 2/3 majority of the both the Houses of Parliament to pass resolution. If the 2/3 majority is not passing resolution to that effect endorsing the proclamation order and on the expiry of two months period, 45th day should be treated as a mandatory date for election.

# 7

# Conclusions

From these analysis, it is found that with these suggestions article 356 can continue to exist as heretofore subject to judicial review as mentioned above. If such suggestions are incorporated it is definite there will be no possibility of abusing of drastic power given under article 356. Moreover, it will also achieve a most acceptable accommodation of the institution of judicial review without eroding the broad scheme of the separation of powers, namely of legislature, executive and judiciary. In the present submission the scope for judicial review of presidential satisfaction under article 356 is extremely limited. We referred to Banaorilal Sharma's case, a 1945 Privy Council decision based on the Government of India Act, 1935 where the judicial committee felt obliged having regard to the need to observe restrained in matters which implicate the satisfaction of the Head of the Executive at the highest level of policy making, to confine the scope of judicial interference to clear cases of legal mala fide, i.e., cases where there is a fraudulent use of governmental authority for purposes wholly extraneous to and beyond the terms of the grant of power. The Rajasthan assembly dissolution case has not taken the scope of judicial review beyond what is stated in the aforesaid Privy Council decision. It is needed to be emphasized that the basic scheme of article 356 is essentially the same as that set out in the predecessor Govt of

India Act, 1935, section 93, and hence in appreciating and apprising the scope and ambit of article 356 we are guided by the experience gathered in the working of the Govt of India Act. Dr.Ambedkar, said as much in the Constituent Assembly in response to a pointed question Prof.Kunzro as to what criteria the Chairman of the Drafting Committee had in mind to determine in what cases the President may infer that the govt of the state can not be carried on in accordance with the provisions of the constitution. Dr.Ambedkar rightly avoided answering the question because the contingencies calling for the invocation of the power under article 356 can not be encompassed with the framework of a rigid formula. It is unfortunate that the MP High Court judgement has failed to consider the wider issues of policy of a kind wholly inapplicable for judicial appraisal which are inherent in the scheme of article 356. A little closer attention to the Drafting history behind article 356 (Draft Article 278) would reveal that the framers preferred to leave the President's discretion free from restrains which would make the power nugatory. In its original form Draft Article 278 required two things as solution preceded to imposition of President's rule in a State: first a proclamation by the governor that a grave emergency existed in that state whereby its peace and tranquillity were threatened and that the govt. of the state can not be carried on in accordance with the provisions of the constitution. On receipt of the proclamation, the President could assume the powers of the state government. Now, these requirements were deleted and the final version of article 356 closely follows section 93 of the Govt. of India Act, 1935. Article 355 has been inserted to impose a duty on the Union to protect the state against external aggression or internal disturbance and also to ensure that govt. of the state is carried on in accordance with the constitution. Surely, if there is a serious break down of law and order even in a part of the state, the Centre can intervene under article 356. It is not necessary that the law and order situation is such as to threaten the peace and tranquillity of the state. Further, the mere fact that article 356 is in a chapter of the constitution that deals with emergency, does not warrant a view taken by the MP High Court in Patwa's case that emergent circumstances involved in large violence or breaches of peace on an extensive scale must exist. Article 356 has attracted also two situations whereby reason of politics of defections or otherwise the govt. may not command the majority on the floor of the assembly and it is not likely to endure for the full term. Infact, in majority of the cases, article 356 has been employed on the ground of governmental instability in the state and has nothing to do with emergency in the sense of Article 352 or 355. Established Precedents clearly show that what is open for the judicial review is the nexus between the actual decision and the grounds invoked which of course must exist in fact. The sufficiency of the material as a basis for warranting presidential satisfaction is in the subjective domain of the Central Government and it is clearly beyond judicial review. It is rather unfortunate that the MP High Court has confused the issue of existence of grounds prima facie, with sufficiency of those grounds and thereby substituted its satisfaction on those grounds for that of the President. In so doing the court has acceded to scope of its authority to review article 356 related decision and entered in the forbidden field of political thicket. It is true our constitution does not recognise what was till recent times a fashionable jargon in the vocabulary of US Constitution - the political question doctrine but the repudiation of the doctrine in the Indian context does not enable the high court to subvert established notions of judicial review to enable it to reach and address issues unmet for judicial pronounced even on the basis of an extended interpretation of judicial power. The MP High Court judgment makes a pointed reference to Chief Justice Chandra Chud observations in A.K.Roy's case AIR 1982 where his Lordship has stated that in 1977 when the assembly dissolution case was decided, article 356 clause 5 as it then stood had made the President's satisfaction clearly non-justiciable. The said exclusionary clause was deleted by the Court 44th Amendment Act. But this in the present submission was done to avoid any possible mis-apprehension to the permissibility of judicial review of presidential proclamation under article 356 in view of the position taken in the dissolution case and in prior case law that legal mala fides are opened for judicial scrutiny. Moreover, judicial review in the sense of the power of the Supreme Court to pass up on questions as to whether the govt. has acted within the constitutional limits to powers being a basic future of the constitution, at any rate, as a fall out of the Keshvanand, pronouncements are enforced upon. Otherwise, it is nothing but used ammunition.

Moore in 'The Justiciability of Challenges to The Use of Military Forces Abroad', 10 Va.J. International Law 85, 95-96 (1969): said "Since these constitutional claims are intended to resolve a dispute about the relative role of Congress and the Executive and not to apply some constitutional prohibition limiting total governmental power to act, such as the Bill of Rights, if there are institutional checks other than judicial determination which each branch exercises on the other it is certainly relevant to the abstention decision. Once a major commitment of troops abroad has been made, Congress could refuse to appropriate funds or to conscript the necessary troops, could censure the President as the House did President Polk for his Mexican War activities, or could even institute impeachment proceedings against the President. And short of these checks, Congress can hold public hearings and mobilize public opinion in a manner which can have a major impact on Executive discretion." In continuation of it, Hughes states that "if the President rejects Congress assertion of authority, what is the likelihood that he will abide by the Court's 'resolution of the dispute?'.

Thus, in view of the above mentioned points of view it will be more important to note that the judiciary while interpreting the provisions particularly in the political questions every caution and concern should be there and if that self restrained approach is allowed to let loose probably taking the risk of credibility itself. The MP High Court judgment is unfortunately made subject to this criticism. As Prof.Raz said, 'Most law making decisions are concerned with extending existing doctrines, successively adjusting them to gradually changing technological, economic, or social conditions and introducing small alterations to avoid the undesirable and unintended consequences of applying rules to circumstances which were not foreseen when those rules were laid down. Such maintenance, repair, and conservation are the function of much legislated law as well. In this respect, there is no substantial difference between precedent and legislation. But there is already a difference in the public image of these institutions. In thinking of legislation one tends to think more of its innovative, reforming role then of its conserving role, which is more prominent in our image of the courts law making rule. "p.200, The Authority of Law, Clarendon Press Oxford, 1983.

The MP High Court attempted to give a new interpretation stating that article 355 is intended to be supplementary to article 356. This kind of interpretation has not only failed to evoke proper precedents but also failed to invoke reasoning. Article 355 and article 356 could be related but where there is a clause of "or otherwise" which is definitely independent of every other provisions as far as the President proclaims emergency under article 356 and imposes President's rule in a state.

Further in this judgment it is also referred that the law and order situation in Bombay and other places which are definitely could be avoided. The judicial interpretation should always be restricted to the point of contention of the litigant parties and better avoid inventing reasons and events which occurred elsewhere like there was law and order situation in Bombay and other places. Probably, this amounts to a kind of judicial involvement in interpreting law and order situations. This is definitely not to be held that will ever fail to generate ill will and diffidence in the minds of people on the credibility of the judiciary. Moreover, to deviate from the existing interpretation of the article 356 do not find favour if the approach of Prof.J. Raz mentioned above is taken into account since there is nothing unforeseen about the likelihood of abuse or use of emergency powers which are incorporated under article 356 or even article 352 and article 360. Therefore, there can be no argument to substantiate that the deviation is necessitated as the founder fathers of this constitution that they were not ware of it. It may be permitted to refer the words of Franklin D. Roosevelt mentioned in the book of Some Half-Hidden Aspects of Indian Social Justice, V.R Krishna Iyer J., Eastern Book Company, Lucknow, 1979, "We want a Supreme Court which will do justice under the constitution-not over it. In our courts we want a govt. of laws". Further, justice V.R. Krishna Iyer referred to the words of Pandit Nehru as "No Supreme Court and no judiciary can stand in judgement over the sovereign will of Parliament representing the will of the entire community. If we go wrong here and there, it can point out, but in the ultimate analysis, where the future of the community is concerned, no judiciary can come in the way. And if it comes in the way, ultimately the whole constitution is a creature of Parliament...... it is obvious that no court, no system of judiciary can function in the nature of a third house, as a kind of third house of correction." Therefore, in the wisdom of justice, judiciary necessarily has to be more concern and caution before they enter into prohibited areas as Untwala J. said in the case of Rajasthan.

Nevertheless, it is not advocated that there should be complete abdication and allow the Parliament or Executive to violate constitutional provisions. Within the constitution, under the constitutional provisions, the judiciary is the custodian and guardian and therefore, the judiciary has to function within the ambit of its limitation. It is very appropriate to state that the liberate interpretation of the judiciary of India has been wholeheartedly accepted. For example, due process clause of United States of America has not been incorporated but procedure established by law in the judicial review article of 13. But, however, in the constitutional decisions of E.P. Rayappa vs Tamil Nadu, 1974, 2 S.C.R.348, (74) A.Sc.555, Maneka Gandhi vs UoI 1978 2 S.C.R. 621, 78 A.Sc.597 and Airport Authorities case - R.D.shetty vs. Airport Authority 1979 3 S.C.R. 1014, 79 A.Sc. and Ajay Hasia vs. Khalid Mujib 1981 A.Sc.487 the due process clause has been incorporated to arrive at judicial decisions. These decisions are welcomed and accepted by the people at large. Similarly, on the legislative limitation on the Parliament on amending the constitution the decision of the Keshvanand Bharati case wherein the Supreme Court has profounded doctrine of basic structure Theory and the same has been accepted. But, however, the decision of the Golakhnath case which denied to parliament the right to amend the constitution was not recognised and accepted eventhough the judicial pronouncement was not that sharper and critical as that of Keshvanand Bharati case. Invoking the judicial decision of Keshvanand Bharati's case many provisions of the constitutional amendments had been strucked off as found in the Minvera Mills case and so on. Therefore, what is more important is not the abdication of judicial function but upgradation of judicial justice. Let the judiciary remain above the board of all so that there is more faith and credibility glittering in the judicial decisions.

## ANNEXURE - EXTRACT OF THE JUDGEMENT OF SUNDER LAL PATWA VS UOI OF JABALPUR BENCH

Having considered the rival contentions of the learned counsel appearing for parties before us and on close examination of the contents of the reports of the governor as also the documents accompanying with them, we are of the opinion that the satisfaction reached by the President in the case before us, on the advise of the Cabinet, is based on the circumstances not relevant for invoking article 356 of the Constitution of India.

As has been explained by us above, such internal disturbance alone, which has actually resulted or has potentiality to result in "failure of constitutional machinery in the state", so as to disable the state from functioning in accordance with the constitution, can be a valid basis of a proclamation of presidential rule and the consequent dissolution of the assembly. Incidents of less or more magnitude of arson, looting and killings, as a reaction to Masjid demolition at Ayodhya, had disturbed several parts of the states in the country, giving rise to necessity of gearing up the law and order machinery, in the affected states to restore peace and harmony. This was so in the state of M.P. as also in other states like Gujarat and Maharashtra.

The Union of India has not been able to support on any material produced before us the imposition of the President's rule only in the states ruled by Bhartiya Janta party. We are informed that in Himanchal Pradesh, where also the Bhartiya Janta party ruled, there were no disturbance whatsoever of the types described to have taken place in the state of M.P. and the imposition of the President's rule in that state was wholly un-called for.

There was no occasion to raise any inference of failure of constitutional machinery under article 365 of the constitution, because there were no central directives, which were disobeyed or disrespected by the state of M.P. In the reports of the governor, there is no specification of alleged deeds or misdeed of the state government in meeting the law and order situation in the state. More worsening of law and order situation in a state due to sudden outbreak of violence, does not call for extreme step of imposition of President's rule unless to the satisfaction of the President, the law and order situation in a state, due to sudden disturbances, has made it or likely to make the functioning of the Government impossible in the state. The central intervention in such an extreme difficult situation may be justified by deploying the army in the affected are or by extending help to the state by sending its reserved force. Although article 257-A, permitting the deployment of army by the Central Government in a state, has been repealed by the 44th Amendment, but the executive power of the Union extends to the legislative field in List-I, Entry 2-A of the Seventh schedule to the constitution, which permits deployment of army or reserved force of the Union in a state in aid of its civil power.

Incapacity or helplessness of a state to meet a threat to public order or peace is not a permissible ground unless it results in non-functioning of the government in the state. In fact, article 355 of the constitution enjoins upon the Union to help the state in maintaining its government. That due is not to be discharged only be proclaiming the presidential rule.

"Internal disturbance", which fails short of resulting into `failure of the constitutional machinery' in the state so as to make it impossible to function, is not intended in the Constitution to be a valid ground for making complete inreads by the Union by taking over completely all executive and legislative wings of a state. The learned commentator Basu in his Silver Jubilee Edition of his book "Commentary on the Constitution of India" Vol.O, has the following comments to make :-

" The broad category of improper use of the extraordinary power is - where it is used for political purpose against a State government which does not belong to the party in power at the Union or to secure the purposes of that party in forming a government of their own in a particular state, taking advantage of fortuitous circumstances."

The constitution of India is a mixture of unitary and federal form of government. It is federal in peace and unitary in times of war, emergency and grave situations, such as, failure of constitutional machinery envisaged in article 356 of the constitution. As has been commented by the learned commentator Basu, "failure of constitutional machinery" means such as "breakdown, which calls for immediate resort to article 356, because the situation is such that it cannot be remedied by any other means."

After more than 40 years of independence, the constitutional democracy in India is reaching a stage of maturity. The possibility of government of different ideologies and complexions being formed in different states and at the Centre is becoming a reality, which was foreseen by the constitution makers. The democracy in India can be described as successful when the government headed by political parties of different ideologies in different states and the Union are allowed to smoothly function within the framework of the constitution for achieving the constitutional goals. This mixed type of 'cooperative federalism' envisaged in the constitutional set up has to be protected to maintain the sound constitutional and democratic traditions. The role of judiciary in a growing democratic society is greater because being a non-political branch of the government of a nation, it is its bounden duty to maintain and enforce the standards of conduct expected of the constitutional functionaries by the founding fathers of the constitution.

The learned counsel appearing for the Union heavily relied on **In A.Sreeramulu** (AIR 1974 A.P.106) in which the exceptional circumstances justifying invocation of article 356 of the constitution have been mentioned to include the situation where a state ministry fails to meet an extraordinary situation, such as, out-break of unprecedented violence. But even in such cases, the attitude of the Union is expected to be one of assistance as the first step, as envisaged by article 355, and article 356 can be invoked only as last resort, such as, where the state government refused to cooperate or had flouted the directions issued by the Union to alleviate the distress. The Andhra Pradesh decision (supr) is to some extent helpful but is a case prior to 14th Amendment Act of the Constitution and is also distinguishable on facts. In the Andhra Pradesh case, the working of government was paralysed by a large scale strikes of the government employees and agitation by the public.

The Governor in his letter has mentioned the 'acts of omissions and commissions' on the part of the State, but has failed to specify them. Reference has also been made by him to the dilemma of the chief minister due to the ban on RSS imposed under the provisions of the Unlawful Activities (Prevention) Act, 1967. The governor has nowhere mentioned that the government, at any point of time, had actually failed to implement the ban on RSS.

The learned Solicitor General argued that the resident could act not only on governor's report, but on any other information received from other sources. It is further argued that the President is protected from being completed to disclose such 'other information' received by him to the court in discharge of his constitutional functions. As has been held by the Supreme Court in 'Rajasthan Case', the satisfaction of the President has to be, in the scheme of the constitution, based on the aid and advise of the cabinet. The decision to impose the President's rule is virtually taken by the cabinet and the action of the President is subject to judicial review in a court. Although the President cannot be made a party in a court of law, the Union Government representing the cabinet can claim no privilege or protection against the disclosure of such", otherwise information" in its possession and which was made the basis of proclamation. As has been held above, the presidential proclamation issued under article 356 is open to judicial review on the settled principles and limits within which any other administrative action of the government is so reviewable. This is the effect of the lifting of the bar on judicial review, by deletion of clause (5), of article 356 by the 44th Amendment Act which was introduced by 39th Amendment Act to the constitution.

The Governor's reports on the worsening of the law and order situation in Bhopal and two other cities of M.P. as aftermath of Ayodhya incident, could not in itself constitute a relevant material having reasonable nexus for the satisfaction of the President in imposing his rule in the state of M.P. There is no other material in existence - either in the report of the governor or from any other sources - to hold that the government in the state of M.P......... on in accordance with the constitution and that there is failure of the constitutional machinery in the State.

It is hard to accept, as argued by the learned Solicitor General, that failure on the part of the government to save the lives and properties of citizens in few cities in the state, as a result of sudden out-break of violence, could reasonable lead to the satisfaction of the President that the Government was unable to function in accordance with the constitution of India and this court cannot sit on judgment over the name.

The presidential proclamation, therefore, for the reasons given by us above, dereserves to be quashed being on invalid exercise of power under article 356 of the constitution.

The next ground urged on behalf of the Union of India is that the proclamation having been approved after full consideration of all circumstances and deliberations by the two Houses of the Parliament is beyond the scrutiny of the court. The learned counsel appearing for the petitioner in his counter-reply submitted that the presidential proclamation issued was not on valid ground and within the scope of article 356 of the constitution. The approval of the two Houses of the Parliament could not validate such an invalid proclamation. The counsel for the petitioner referred to the following passage from the Third Edition of ~Practice and Procedure of Parliament" by M.N. Kaul and S.L. Shakdhar at pages 534 and 535, which reads as under:

" The .... of a proclamation, unless revoked earlier by the President, is two months. There is no provision under which Parliament can cut it short. It is only if the proclamation is to continue in force beyond two months that Parliament has to approve of it in a manner similar to that in the case of a proclamation of emergency.

It has been held that an amendment to the resolution ...... to approve the President's proclamation is out of order if there ..... is negative in character or is beyond the scope of the resolution, or is contradictory to the text of the resolution. An amendment seeking to give conditional approval to the proclamation is also inadmissible.

The House may either adopt or not adopt a resolution which seeks to approve the proclamation. The resolution before the House cannot take any other form. As such, no amendments/substitute .... can be moved to such a resolution. A resolution seeking disapproval of the proclamation is inadmissible as there is no provision under article 356 for such a resolution."

On the effect of grant of approval to the proclamation by the Parliament, the contention advanced by the Union of India does not appear to be acceptable. The proclamation, in any case, is valid for a period of two months under sub-article (3) of article 356 of the constitution and it is so irrespective of its approval or disapproval by the two Houses of Parliament. Its life for a period of two months cannot be cut short by the Parliament. The constitutional provision in article 356 sub-clause (3) of the constitution is very clear in that respect. The approval of the Parliament, merely gives the proclamation further lease of life for six months. The Parliament, therefore, in approving or disapproving the proclamation does not sit in judgment over the satisfaction of the President reached on the advise of the Central Cabinet for imposing the presidential rule for two months. But the Parliament only considers the desirability of the proclamation being continued beyond two months. The approval granted by the two Houses of Parliament, therefore, does not amount to approving or disapproving the presidential proclamation, which, in any event, is valid for a period of two months. The action of the President in imposing its rule in a state and dissolution of the assembly is irreversible. Disapproval of the proclamation by the Parliament can also have no such effect of restoring the position ante, i.e., of resuscitation the already dissolved Assembly. The presidential proclamation issued, therefore, for an initial period of two months can neither be validated or invalidated by the Parliament by its approval or disapproval. The contention advanced to the contrary by the learned counsel for the Union of India, therefore, has to be rejected.

The last question, which remains to be decided, is about the desirability and validity of the dissolution of the Assembly by the impugned proclamation. The learned ex Advocate General, Shri N.C.Jain, contended that the alleged internal disturbances in the State and the failure of the executive branch of the Government to deal with it satisfactorily, furnished no justification for dissolving the assembly, which could be allowed to remain intact or in suspended animation. His line of argument was towards indicating that the proclamation intends, in fact, to achieve the political advantage of taking a fresh election in the State.

We have held above that the proclamation was invalid and beyond the scope of article 356 of the constitution. It is, therefore, not necessary for us to decide the question of justification of dissolution of the assembly. The entire proclamation, in our opinion, being based on the grounds not material and warranted for invoking the extraordinary powers of the President under article 356 of the constitution, the proclamation and along with it the action of dissolving the Assembly, should fall with it.

As a result of the discussion aforesaid and the conclusions drawn, the petition succeeds and is hereby allowed. The presidential proclamation dated 15.12.1992 (Annexure-A) is hereby quashed. All consequential effects thereon shall follow. In the circumstances, we make no order as to costs. The amount of security deposited by the petition be refunded to him.

CHIEF JUSTICE JUDGE JUDGE

2.4.1993